A
GOURMET'S
GUIDE TO

DRIED FRUIT
AND
NUTS

A GOURMET'S GUIDE TO

DRIED FRUIT AND NUTS

CAROLE HANDSLIP
FELICITY JACKSON

Photography by
SUE ATKINSON

HPBooks
a division of
PRICE STERN SLOAN
Los Angeles

This book was created by Merehurst Limited
Ferry House, 51/57 Lacy Road, London SW15 1PR

© Salamander Books Ltd., 1991

HPBooks
A division of Price Stern Sloan, Inc.
Los Angeles, California
Printed in Belgium by Proost International Book Production, Turnhout

9 8 7 6 5 4 3 2 1

Library of Congress Cataloging-in-Publication Data

Handslip, Carole.
    A gourmet's guide to dried fruits and nuts / by Carole Handslip,
Felicity Jackson.
        p.   cm.
    ISBN 0-89586-852-0
    1. Cookery (Dried Fruit) 2. Cookery (Nuts) 3. Dried fruit.
4. Nuts.   I. Jackson, Felicity.   II. Title.
TX826.5H36   1991
641.6'4—dc20   90-34780
                                                                CIP

Notice: The information contained in this book is true and complete to
the best of our knowledge. All recommendations are made without any
guarantees on the part of the author or Price Stern Sloan. The author
and publisher disclaim all liability in connection with the use of this
information.

This book is printed on acid-free paper.

Commissioned and Directed by Merehurst Limited
Photography: Sue Atkinson
Food Stylist: Maria Kelly
Home Economist: Carole Handslip
Color reproduction by Kentscan, England

ACKNOWLEDGMENTS

The publishers would like to thank Epicure, Petty Wood & Co. Ltd.,
Central Way, Andover, Hants, and Hider Food Imports, Witshire Rd,
Hull, for supplying dried fruit and nuts for photography.

Contents

Introduction

Dried fruit and nuts are so convenient—always on hand to use for all kinds of sweet and savory dishes, or simply to nibble as healthy snacks. Fully illustrated throughout, this book helps you identify at a glance all the different types of dried fruit and nuts available. There is plenty of information on how to prepare and use them, too.

Discover how to dry fruit at home—not as difficult as it sounds—or try preparing your own candied fruit for Christmas.

In the recipe section you will find exciting new dried fruit ideas—from Moroccan Lamb Stew and Calves' Liver with Apple, to tempting desserts, such as Mango Brûlée with Nut Curls and Summer Fruits & Peach Coulis. Dried fruit gives cakes a deliciously moist texture—just sample the Pear & Chocolate Cake or Fig & Banana Slices.

Nuts in various guises are used to add flavor and texture to all manner of recipes, including soups, like Cashew & Fennel; main courses, such as Turbot with Pine Nuts; and mouthwatering desserts and, of course, cakes and pastries—try Portuguese Almond Cake or Apricot & Pistachio Rolls.

This comprehensive book will prove invaluable to anyone interested in creating imaginative recipes from dried fruit and nuts.

Dried Fruit

The idea of drying fruit was first discovered by the ancient Egyptians. They noticed that ripe grapes mistakenly left on the vine became exceptionally sweet as the sun dried them out. When picked, these grapes kept without going moldy; so they began sun-drying other fruit. Dried fruits are illustrated in Egyptian wall paintings from the time of the Pharaohs and were included in Egyptian royal tombs along with all the other worldly treasures. In classical Greece dried fruit was valued as a preventative medicine.

In Middle Eastern and Mediterranean countries people still dry fruit in the sun on their flat rooftops. In California and Australia, where fruit drying is now a thriving industry, most of the fruit is dried in special dehydration units.

Drying is a convenient way of storing fruit so that it is available at any time of the year, regardless of whether the fresh version is in season or not.

To produce good quality dried fruit, it must be picked when fully ripe. The fruit is dried naturally in the hot sun or in special units such as hot air tunnels, which blast the fruit with hot air until most of the moisture has evaporated, leaving highly concentrated natural sugars which prevent bacteria growth and thus preserve the fruit.

Buying & Storing Dried Fruit

All dried fruit sold in retail shops should have a "best before" date on the label. Although dried fruit can last for many months it is best to choose the freshest possible, so buy from a shop with a good turnover.

Choose plump, unblemished fruit. Mixed fruit can be bought, but it is usually better to buy packages of individual fruits as they are often fresher.

Check the package labels for additives. The two main ones used in the production of dried fruit are sulfur dioxide and mineral oil.

Certain dried fruits—particularly raisins, apple rings and apricots—are sometimes treated with sulfur dioxide to help prevent bacterial growth and loss of color. The small amount of sulfur dioxide used in dried fruit is generally deemed to be harmless, but in excess this chemical can cause severe allergic reactions. You may consider it worthwhile seeking out fruit that has not been treated. Or you can remove some of the sulfur dioxide by boiling the dried fruit in water to cover for 1 minute, then draining before use.

Sometimes fruits are coated with a mineral oil to give them a glossy appearance and prevent them from sticking together. These mineral oils can adversely affect the body's absorption of certain vitamins and minerals, so it is worth checking the package label to see if one is present. If a mineral oil has been used, you can remove it by carefully washing the fruit in warm water. Some manufacturers use a harmless vegetable oil instead of mineral oil wherever possible.

Dried fruit should be stored away from direct heat and sunlight. It will keep for up to a year but is best used within six months.

Using Dried Fruit

Most dried fruits can be eaten raw as a nutritious snack. They are high in protein, vitamins A, B and C, minerals such as iron and calcium, and dietary fiber. They can be added to sweet and savory dishes, but are particularly useful in desserts, cakes and cookies.

Some dried fruits are sold already washed and need no soaking, although they can be plumped up before use by soaking for a few minutes in hot water if wished. Others need to be rinsed before using.

To reconstitute dried fruit, simply place in a bowl, cover with water and leave for about 6 hours or until plumped up. After soaking, cook the fruit very gently in the soaking liquid until tender.

Jars of dried fruit soaked in alcohol provide delicious desserts for impromptu entertaining.

Raisins dried from grapes

Apricots

Apple

Peaches

Date

The date (*Phoenix dactylifera*) is the fruit of the date palm tree which flourishes in dry tropical countries. Even small amounts of rain result in soggy, tasteless dates, so the best growing lands are the hot, arid deserts. Date palm trees are so sensitive to cold and moisture that they rarely flourish within 25 miles of the sea.

The cultivation of dates is recorded in the Arab lands some 7000 years ago. Today dates are grown commercially in the countries on the North African shores of the Mediterranean—Tunisia and Algeria—and in the Middle Eastern countries of Egypt, Iran and Iraq. They are also grown in California, which boasts some of the finest dates in the world.

Ripe dates are cut from the palm and are either sun-dried or dried in hot air tunnels. They are not sulfured. For storage, the moisture is evaporated to a very low level. When ready for shipment, they are mildly steamed to reconstitute them to a level of about 15% moisture content. Tunisian and Algerian dates are often coated with glucose to help retain their moisture. Others may be treated with mineral oil, but most are not.

Dried dates may be classified as dessert or cooking dates. Although the term cooking denotes fruit of a slightly lower quality, they are still suitable for eating raw.

The best dessert dates are known as *Deglet nour* (fingers of light). They are a golden amber color, often translucent, long, fleshy and soft-textured with thin skins. Many come from California.

Tunisian and Algerian dessert dates are mainly imported into Britain through Marseilles, in France; it is there that they are packed into the familiar boxes seen at Christmas.

Many of the cooking date varieties come from Iran and Iraq. They are cheaper to produce, darker and shorter than dessert dates, with a coarser, more fibrous texture. Many are sold pitted ready for use. Chinese red dates, available from oriental stores, are used in many traditional Chinese desserts. These red dates are actually dried jujubes, not the dried fruit of the date palm.

Pressed dates are also popular for cooking. These are pitted dates and date pieces pressed together into rectangular blocks, then wrapped in cellophane.

Uses
In parts of the Middle East, dates form an essential part of the diet. They need no preparation and can be eaten as a snack, used in cakes, puddings, quick breads, salads, savory rice dishes, jams and chutneys. Pitted dessert dates can be stuffed with almonds or peanuts, or a firm ground nut mixture, to make a tasty snack or cocktail food.

Apple

The apple (*Malus sylvestris*) has been a popular candidate for drying since Shakespeare's time, when dried apples were called applejohns. Nowadays it is the large apple producers like Australia, the United States and South Africa who dry them on a large scale.

Ripe apples are peeled, cored and cut into rings or slices, then dried in hot air tunnels. They are usually sulfured before drying to prevent mold developing and the color darkening.

Uses
Dried apple rings make a tasty, chewy snack—much healthier than sweets as they contain vitamin C, some of the B vitamins and a good supply of minerals. They are also high in dietary fiber.

Chopped apple pieces can be added to cereals, combined with nuts and other dried fruit to make trail mixes, or soaked with other fruit to make excellent compotes, served warm on their own or with yogurt or cream.

Tunisian Dates

California Dates

Pressed Dates

Date pieces

Cooking dates

Chinese red 'dates'

Apple rings

Apple chunks

Apricot

The apricot (*Prunus armeniaca*) is one of the most popular dried fruits and is among the highest in food value, containing vitamins C and B, and significant amounts of iron and calcium. It is also high in fiber.

Originally cultivated in China, apricots were carried by traders to the Middle East and Europe, then by Spanish settlers to California.

Nowadays huge orchards of apricots are grown specifically for drying by the major apricot producing countries such as the United States, Australia, South Africa and Turkey.

Ripe fruit is either pitted without halving, or halved and pitted, before drying. It may or may not be sulfured. The rich golden orange color of the fruit intensifies as the sugar content is concentrated.

Turkey is renowned for its output of whole pitted apricots. Turkish fruit tends to be paler in color and have a milder flavor than the Australian, Californian and South African fruit. Select apricots of a uniform size, with a good orange color and unblemished skins.

Poorer quality fruit is cut into pieces and packed tightly together in bulk—often called pressed apricots.

Hunza apricots: Also known as wild apricots, these have been cultivated by the Hunza tribe in the Himalayas for centuries and are considered by many to be the best dried apricots. They are small, pale brown and unsulfured. Hunza apricots are very hard and must be soaked and cooked before they can be eaten.

Uses

Apart from Hunza apricots, dried apricots can be eaten either as they are, or after soaking. The halved and pitted types make delicious fruit compotes, or they can be chopped and served with yogurt, or added to breakfast cereals and muesli. Chopped apricots add a delicious tangy flavor to cakes and quick breads, puddings, rice salads, curries and stuffings for meat and poultry. Pressed apricots are mostly used for making jams and chutneys.

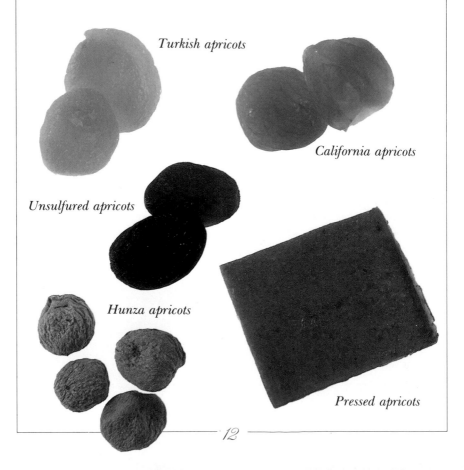

Turkish apricots

California apricots

Unsulfured apricots

Hunza apricots

Pressed apricots

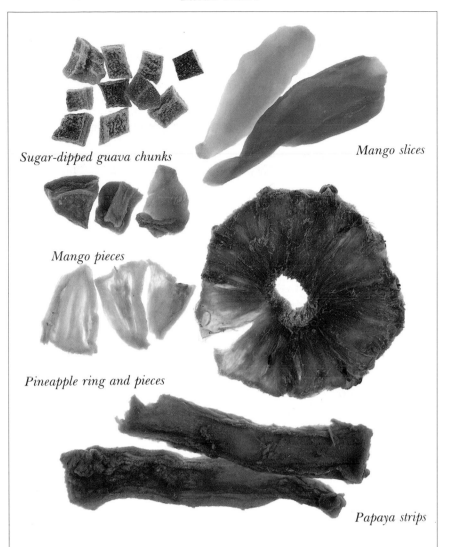

Sugar-dipped guava chunks

Mango slices

Mango pieces

Pineapple ring and pieces

Papaya strips

Tropical Fruit

A variety of dried tropical fruits can be found in ethnic and health food shops, but they tend to be more expensive than other dried fruits. Trail mixes containing a mixture of tropical fruits are widely available.

Papaya: The avocado-shaped papaya or pawpaw (*Carica papaya*) grows among the huge leaves of a tropical tree. In dried form, papaya is often sold in long strips. It is also available as sugar-dipped chunks. The fruit is high in vitamin C, potassium and dietary fiber and makes an excellent snack on its own. It can also be soaked and mixed with other fruits in compotes.

Pineapple: Pineapple (*Ananas comosus*) in dried form is sold in pieces, chunks or rings, some sugar-dipped.

Like the fresh fruit, dried pineapple contains vitamins A and C, and the mineral potassium.

Chopped dried pineapple adds an exotic touch to trail mixes, muesli, quick breads, puddings and savory grain dishes. Unsweetened pineapple makes a good healthy snack for children.

Mango: Dried mangoes (*Mangifera indica*) are available in long slices, which are very sweet, or chunks which may be sugar-dipped. The fruit can be chopped and added to curries, sweet and sour dishes, puddings, cakes, jams and chutneys.

Guava: Guavas (*Psidium guajava*) are also available in dried form, in slices, which are sweet, and chunks which may be sugar-dipped.

Peach & Nectarine

Peach trees are known to have grown in China as far back as the 10th century B.C. Today the main dried peach producers are Australia, California and South Africa, with some coming from China.

There are two different types of peach (*Prunus persica*): the cling, with a pit that grows as an integral part of the fruit and is difficult to remove; and the freestone, which has a pit that can easily be removed when the fruit is halved. Farmers growing peaches for drying prefer the freestone type.

To dry, the fruit is halved and pitted. Cling peaches are usually peeled while freestone peaches have their skins left on. Peaches are often sulfured before they are dried in the sun. After drying, Chinese peaches may be dipped in glucose syrup to prevent them from drying out further during storage.

Nectarines are dried in the same way as peaches, although less drying time is required as they are smaller.

Both peaches and nectarines have a rich, strong flavor and can be used in exactly the same way as apricots (see page 12), although they tend to be more expensive.

Pear

The pear (*Pyrus communis*) is one of the lesser known dried fruits, but dried pears are quite delicious and well worth looking for. The main producers are California, Australia and South Africa, with China becoming an important source. Most of the pears that are dried are the Bartlett type.

As fully ripe pears are easily damaged, they are usually picked by hand. The fruit may be left whole, peeled or unpeeled, or it may be halved and the core removed. Pears are usually sulfured before being dried.

Dried pears from China may be coated in glucose syrup to prevent them from drying further during storage.

Uses

Dried pears make a good snack just as they are, or they can be soaked and used to make compotes. Chopped pears can be added to puddings, cakes, savory rice and meat dishes as well as jams and chutneys. If using whole dried pears, remove the cores, skins and seeds after soaking.

Banana

Banana producers tend to concentrate most of their efforts on the fresh fruit. Dried bananas are therefore not as widely available as other dried fruits, although they can usually be found in good health food shops and ethnic stores.

Bananas (*Musa sapientum*) are dried in their skins, then peeled and packed in long blocks. During drying, the fruit turns a dark brown color, making the finished product look quite unappealing. Don't be put off by this—the strong distinctive flavor of dried bananas is especially good in cakes and quick breads, curries and chutneys. They also make an ex-

cellent snack eaten on their own.

Although dried bananas store well in a dry place, they tend to develop a sugary appearance after 6 to 12 months.

Banana chips: These are very thin slices of unripe banana, fried in an oil and sugar or honey mixture, and dried. They retain their golden yellow color but have only a mild, rather sugary flavor. Unlike other dried fruit, banana chips are crunchy and are generally not suitable for use in cooking. They are best as a snack, or as part of a trail mix.

Peaches

Nectarines

Pears

Bananas

Banana chips

Fig

The fig (*Ficus carica*) has been a popular dried fruit for thousands of years, dating back to the ancient civilizations of Rome, Greece and Arabia. Believed to have originated in Turkey, figs then spread throughout the Middle East to China and India.

Turkey is still a major supplier of dried figs, though during the First World War, when Turkish figs were prevented from reaching Europe, Californian growers developed large orchards to supply the European market.

Ripe fruit is dried in the sun for several days, then dipped in boiling water. Some figs are given a coating of glucose syrup to help preserve the moisture content.

Whole dried figs may be packed upright in a circular shape like a wheel or pressed into rectangular blocks. They may also be packed in semicircular fan shapes.

Figs often have a white sugary crusting on the surface; this is caused by the sugars in the fruit crystallizing and permeating through to the surface.

Uses

Figs make a very healthy snack food. They are an excellent source of dietary fiber and contain small amounts of vitamin A, some of the B vitamins, and calcium, iron, potassium and phosphorus.

They can be soaked and poached in fruit juice or wine with added spices and made into a compote with other dried fruits, or they can be added to stir-fried savory dishes, particularly vegetable ones.

Figs can be chopped and used in fruit cakes and puddings to give a stronger flavor than the traditional currants and raisins.

Prune

Prunes (*Prunus domestica*) are a dried variety of purple-skinned plum grown specifically for drying—the plum will not ferment if dried without being pitted. The most important producer is California.

Prunes are most valued for their laxative properties—they are one of the richest sources of dietary fiber. They are also high in vitamin A and provide modest amounts of the B vitamins as well as the minerals potassium, iron, phosphorus and magnesium.

Prunes are dried whole, pitted or unpitted. Some are sun-dried but many are dried using hot air tunnels. The dried prunes are usually treated with a preservative called potassium sorbate (sorbic acid) to prevent mold forming on them.

Prunes are graded according to size with the best labelled jumbo or extra large. Tenderized prunes that do not

need soaking are becoming more widely available.

To soften prunes, cover with fruit juice or cold tea and leave to soak overnight; simmer gently in the soaking liquid for a few minutes, until tender.

Uses

Serve whole prunes with yogurt, or slice and add to fruit salads or use for stuffings. Fill whole pitted prunes with almonds, cashews or a nut paste and serve as a cocktail snack. Prunes—stuffed or plain—wrapped in bacon and grilled are delicious.

Chopped prunes make a good substitute for raisins in yeast breads, quick breads and cookies.

Tenderized prunes do not need soaking. They can be eaten as they are as a snack, or simmered for a few minutes if using for compotes or similar desserts.

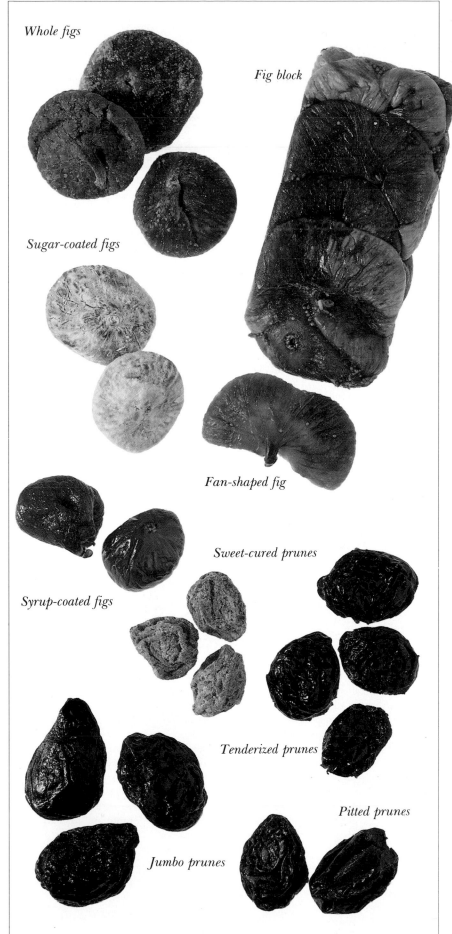

Whole figs

Fig block

Sugar-coated figs

Fan-shaped fig

Sweet-cured prunes

Syrup-coated figs

Tenderized prunes

Pitted prunes

Jumbo prunes

Grapes

Different varieties of vines produce different types of grapes with their own characteristic appearance and taste. Not all of these grapes can be dried successfully; they have to contain enough fruit sugar to ensure they will be juicy when the water in them has evaporated. Dried grapes (*Vitis vinefera*) are divided into currants, raisins and golden raisins.

Currants: These are dried from a variety of black grape originating in Corinth. They are tiny, seedless, very sweet and always sold unsulfured. Most currants come from Greece and Crete; Australia and the United States are the other main producers.

The currant vine is a smaller, bushier vine than that of the raisin; it thrives in poor rocky soil which is rich in minerals.

Currants are one of the few foods that do not fall into the "biggest is best" category—biggest is definitely not best! A currant that is allowed to become too large will develop a small seed which is often mistaken for grit or dirt when the fruit is eaten. The traditional currant growers of Greece and Crete prevent a seed developing by cutting a ring of bark from the stem of each vine once the grapes reach a certain stage of maturity. The sap cannot then rise and this prevents further development—the grape continues to ripen without growing larger.

Although all currants come from Corinth grapes, the quality of the dried fruit can vary according to the area in which they were grown and the method of drying.

Look for the word Vostizza on currants; these are luscious black fruit with a fine bloom and sweet flavor. Poorer quality currants may vary in color—a reddish appearance means they were dried too quickly in the sun.

Currants are graded into small and medium: small ones are used mainly in baking, while the fleshier medium-size fruit is perfect for mincemeat, puddings, cakes and savory dishes, or as a snack.

Raisins: These are dried white grapes. If they are not a seedless type, they may be dried with or without the seeds in. Those dried with their seeds in but having them removed before packing are known as seeded raisins.

Although they come from pale grapes, raisins darken as they dry. They come in a variety of colors, sizes and flavors.

Muscats from the United States are very dark brown with a strong flavor. They are seeded after drying. *Capes* from South Africa are dark brown and sweet. They also have the seeds removed after drying. Australian *lexias* are light brown with a sweet flavor. They are seeded after drying and are usually coated with vegetable oil.

Valencias from Spain are light brown, usually pitted, with a full fruity flavor. They are usually sulfured. Some seedless valencias are also available—these are the smaller grapes from the tip of the cluster which do not form seeds.

Muscatels are prime dessert raisins produced by Australia, Spain and South Africa. They are large with a purplish-brown skin. Muscatels are dried in clusters still on the stalks, with their seeds in, and are packed and sold like this.

Raisins should generally be sorted before using; if rinsed, dry thoroughly if using in a cake mixture or the cake may sink. Raisins can be eaten as a snack or used in salads, other savory dishes, pudding, cakes, pickles and chutneys.

Golden raisins: These are dried seedless white grapes. Golden and succulent, they are larger than currants, smaller than most raisins, and sweeter than both.

The main producers of golden raisins are Australia, Turkey, Greece and Crete. Some golden raisins are sulfured and coated with mineral oil to give them a shiny appearance; others, notably from Australia, are unsulfured and treated with vegetable oil instead of mineral oil.

Use golden raisins as you would currants and dark raisins.

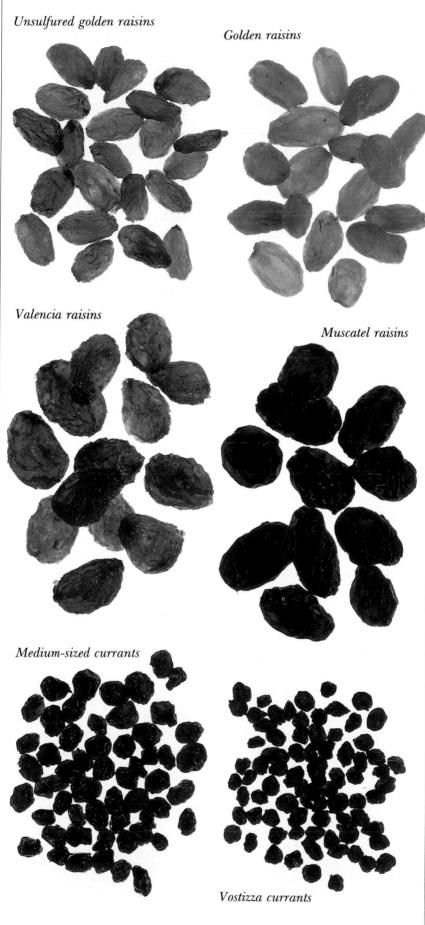

Unsulfured golden raisins

Golden raisins

Valencia raisins

Muscatel raisins

Medium-sized currants

Vostizza currants

Drying Fruit at Home

Apple rings, pear slices, nectarines and pineapple rings

Many fruits can be dried successfully at home in a low oven or one of the small dehydrators for home use. Use only perfectly fresh ripe fruit as this has a better flavor and retains its color better than unripe fruit; it also dries much more quickly. Apples, apricots, pears, peaches and pineapples are good choices.

Preparing the Fruit
Apples: Peel and cut into rings, or wedges, if preferred. Put in a bowl of salted water—2 teaspoons salt to 5 cups water—for a few minutes to prevent discoloration. Shake off excess water.
Peaches, nectarines, apricots, plums: Remove pits carefully and leave whole or halve.
Pears: Leave whole (cored or uncored) or cut into quarters or eighths. Like apples, they are best dipped in salt water before drying.
Pineapple: Peel, core and cut into rings.

Drying the Fruit
Heat the oven to warm or lowest setting 120F (50C) to start with; this can be increased to about 140F (60C) when the fruit has been drying for a while.

It is essential to heat the fruit very slowly, otherwise the outside of the fruit will harden and prevent the moisture inside from evaporating. Plums, especially, must not be dried at too high a temperature or the skins will burst and the juice will be lost too quickly, making the fruit unpleasantly tough.

Spread fruit in a single layer on wire racks covered with muslin or cheesecloth to prevent wire marking the fruit. If using new cheesecloth, wash it first. If preferred, thread apple rings on bamboo skewers and lay across the rack. Leave in the oven, with the door open, until fruit appears dry; it is important to leave the door open as air must circulate while the fruit is drying.

Depending on the fruit, the drying can take anything from 4 to 12 hours. If preferred, it can be done in stages over two or three days using the heat from the oven after baking.

Apple rings will resemble chamois leather and be springy if pressed when they are dry enough. Whole plums and apricots are dry enough when they can be squeezed gently without the skin breaking or any of the juice oozing out.

Once the fruit is dried, leave it at room temperature 12 hours to cool, then pack in cardboard or wooden boxes lined with waxed paper; it must *not* be stored in airtight containers. Store in a dry place and use within 6 months.

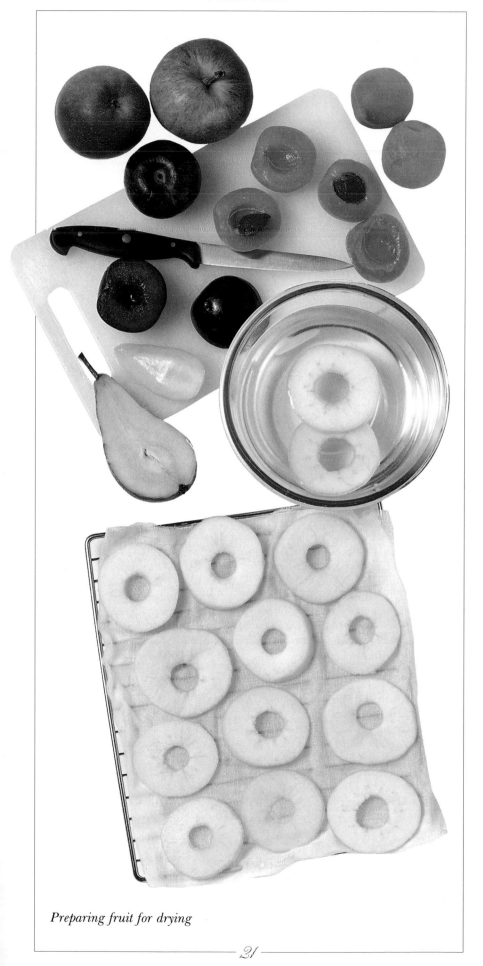

Preparing fruit for drying

Candied Fruit

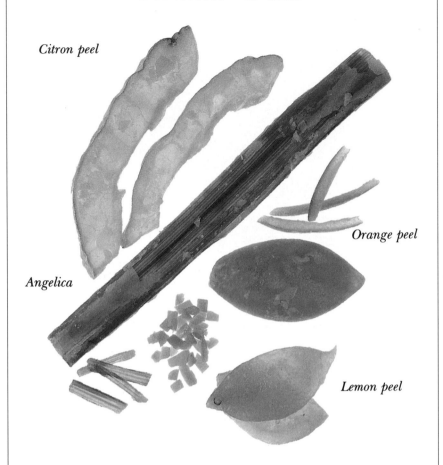

Citron peel

Angelica

Orange peel

Lemon peel

Candied fruit in pretty boxes usually appears in the shops at Christmas. During the rest of the year it is somewhat neglected—largely because it is so expensive. However, candied fruit is relatively cheap to make at home and surprisingly easy to do (see page 24)—you need only 5 minutes a day throughout the preparation period.

Not all fruit can be candied—cherries, grapes, pineapples, apricots, peaches and plums are the most successful to candy, and therefore the most commonly available to buy. Kiwifruit slices, orange and lemon slices, whole gooseberries, kumquats and limequats are also excellent.

Candied citrus peel: Orange, lemon and grapefruit peel is commonly sold chopped and mixed together in containers. Look for whole strips of orange, lemon, citron and grapefruit peel—these are most attractive and delicious.

Candied angelica: Usually sold in small packages or blocks, this is the candied stem of an herb, not a fruit.

Marrons glacés: Whole chestnuts candied in vanilla-flavored syrup are also available—in cans and jars. Mostly imported from France, they tend to be expensive, but marrons glacés can be made at home (see page 31).

Uses

As well as being delicious on their own as a Christmas treat, candied fruits are used for adding flavor to rich cakes, particularly fruit ones; glacé cherries, chopped pineapple, apricots and plums are all delicious in cakes. They can also be used in homemade ice creams or as a decorative topping for soufflés and other desserts.

Candied citrus peel is mostly used in cake mixtures, while angelica is most frequently used as a decoration for cakes and cookies.

Apple slices

Pear halves

Orange slices

Orange

Pineapple pieces

Grape

Lime

Mandarin

Figs

Gooseberries

Apricot

Stawberries

Candying Fresh Fruit

Pineapple pieces, kumquats, kiwifruit slices, guava wedges and lime slices

The candying process is lengthy but very simple. The fruit is covered with a hot sugar syrup to which more and more sugar is added over several days until the water in the fruit has diffused out and the fruit is impregnated with sugar. The process must be gradual; if the sugar were added all at once the fruit would shrivel and toughen. It is this lengthy preparation that makes candied fruit so expensive to buy.

Once the candying process is complete, the fruit is dried and then given either a glacé or crystallized finish. The glacé finish gives a shiny translucent look, while the crystallized finish gives a sugary appearance.

To be suitable for candying, fresh fruit must be firm and fleshy and have a good strong flavor; a delicate flavor will be lost once the fruit is impregnated with sugar. Cherries, grapes, apricots, pineapple, plums and peaches are ideal. Don't expect your candied fruits to look the same as commercially candied ones as it is impossible to achieve the same finish. Home candied fruits have a good flavor.

Preparing the Fruit

Rinse or wipe the fruit. Pit cherries and seed grapes; halve and pit apricots or plums. Peel and halve or quarter larger fruit such as pears or peaches, then remove the pits or cores.

Cook the fruit very gently in water to cover just long enough to make it tender; do not overcook or the fruit will break up, but cook long enough to make it tender or the sugar will not be able to penetrate the fruit and it will end up dark and tough. Small fruit such as cherries need only 3 to 4 minutes, while tougher fruit like apricots may take 10 to 15 minutes. Drain the fruit, reserving the cooking liquid, and place in a shallow dish, large enough to take the fruit in a single layer.

The cooking liquid is then used to make a sugar syrup (see page 26) that will gradually have more and more sugar added to it. If candying more than one fruit, each variety must be candied in a separate syrup or the flavor of the individual fruits will be masked.

Preparing fruit for candying

Making the Sugar Syrup

For 1 pound of fruit, put 1-1/4 cups of the initial cooking liquid in a saucepan (making the liquid up to this quantity with water if necessary).

Add 3/4 cup granulated sugar or 1/4 cup sugar and 4 ounces powdered glucose. Heat gently, stirring until the sugar has dissolved, then bring to a boil. Add any coloring—orange for apricots, red if candying cherries, for example. Pour the syrup over the fruit in the dish.

There should be enough syrup to cover the fruit; if not, make up more syrup of the same strength. It is important to have enough to cover the fruit completely or it will not be properly candied. Cover the fruit with a plate or saucer to keep it submerged in the syrup and leave 24 hours.

Strengthening the Sugar Syrup

On day 2, after the fruit has been steeping in syrup 24 hours, drain off the syrup into a saucepan and add 1/4 cup sugar. Heat gently, stirring until the sugar has dissolved, then bring to a boil. Pour over the fruit. Cover and leave another 24 hours. Repeat this day 2 process five more times (on days 3, 4, 5, 6 and 7).

On day 8, drain off the syrup into a saucepan and add 1/3 cup sugar. Bring to a boil and remove from the heat. Add the fruit, return to the heat and boil gently 3 to 4 minutes. Pour the syrup and fruit back into the dish, cover and leave 48 hours. Repeat this day 8 process (on day 10) then leave 4 days. By day 14 the syrup should look like clear honey.

Drying the Candied Fruit

Drain off the syrup and reserve for using with desserts, such as fruit salads or ice cream

Arrange the fruit on a wire rack placed over a plate or baking sheet to catch the drips and leave to dry in a warm place for 2 to 3 days, or in a very low oven (120F/50C) for several hours. Drying time will vary according to the time of year and the temperature of the drying place. The fruit is dry when it no longer feels sticky. It is then ready for a glacé or crystallized finish (see pages 28-29).

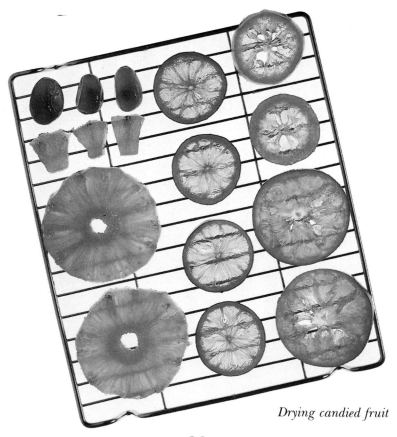

Drying candied fruit

Candying Canned Fruit

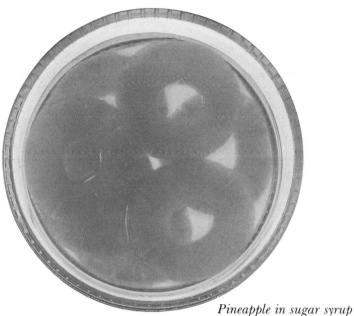

Pineapple in sugar syrup

Canned fruits in syrup are slightly quicker to candy because of the processing they have already gone through. It is also usually cheaper to candy the canned fruit rather than the fresh equivalent. Pineapple, plums, peaches and apricots are the most successful.

The fruit must be of uniform size: pineapple should be in small rings or chunks, and apricots, peaches and plums should be halved. It is not worth candying less than 1 pound of fruit (drained weight).

Drain and reserve the canned syrup. Put the fruit in a shallow heat-proof dish large enough to take the fruit in a single layer.

Making the Sugar Syrup
For 1 pound drained fruit, use 1-1/4 cups of the reserved canned syrup, making it up with water if necessary. Put it in a saucepan and add 1 cup granulated sugar or 1/2 cup sugar and 4 ounces powdered glucose. Heat gently, stirring until the sugar has dissolved, then bring to a boil. Add any coloring, if using, and pour over the fruit. The syrup should cover the fruit completely; if there is not quite enough, make up more syrup using 1 cup sugar to 7/8 cup

water.

If candying several different fruits, put them in separate dishes and keep the syrups separate.

Cover the fruit with a plate or saucer to keep it submerged and leave 24 hours.

Strengthening the Sugar Syrup
On day 2, after the fruit has been steeping 24 hours, drain off the syrup into a saucepan and add 1/4 cup sugar. Heat gently, stirring until the sugar has dissolved, then bring to a boil. Pour over the fruit, cover and leave to stand another 24 hours.

Repeat this day 2 process twice more (on days 3 and 4). On day 5, drain off the syrup and add 1/3 cup sugar. Heat gently, stirring until the sugar has dissolved, then bring to a boil and add the fruit. Bring back to a boil, then simmer 3 to 4 minutes. Pour the fruit and syrup back into the dish and leave 48 hours.

Repeat this day 5 process on day 7, then leave 4 days. By day 11, the syrup should be the consistency of clear honey.

Dry the candied fruit the same way as candied fresh fruit (see page 26). It is then ready for a glacé or crystallized finish (see pages 28-29).

Applying glacé finish to candied fruit

Glacé Finish

For 1 pound dry candied fruit, put 2 cups granulated sugar and 2/3 cup cold water in a saucepan and heat gently, stirring until the sugar has dissolved. Bring to a boil and boil 2 minutes.

In a separate saucepan, bring some water to a boil. Pour a small amount of syrup into a warmed bowl or cup. Keep the remainder hot, covered with a tight-fitting lid to prevent evaporation.

Dip the candied fruit, one piece at a time, into the boiling water for 20 seconds. Shake off excess water and dip into the syrup in the bowl or cup. Put the fruit on a wire rack.

Continue dipping pieces of fruit into the syrup in the bowl or cup until it becomes cloudy, then replace it with fresh syrup from the saucepan. Leave the fruit to dry in a warm place 2 to 3 days or in a very low oven (120F/50C) several hours until it is easy to handle—no longer very sticky.

Crystallized Finish

To give candied fruit a crystallized finish, bring some water to a boil in a saucepan. Spread some granulated or superfine sugar on a piece of waxed paper.

Dip the candied fruit, one piece at a time, into the boiling water. Shake off excess water, then roll each piece in the sugar. Let dry.

Packing & Storing

Pack candied fruit in cardboard or wooden boxes which are not airtight. Do not pack them in airtight plastic containers or they will go moldy.

Stored in a cool, dry place, candied fruit will keep for several months but after that it will start to go hard.

If packing candied fruit as a gift, pack it in a box lined with waxed paper and place waxed paper between the layers of fruit so they do not touch. Alternatively put individual fruits in waxed paper cups. A selection of candied fruit in one box makes an attractive gift, particularly if the pieces are arranged in individual paper cups.

Applying crystallized finish to candied fruit

Candying Citrus Peel

Candying peel is a good way of using up the part of the fruit that would otherwise be thrown away. Orange, lemon and grapefruit peel can be candied together or separately. It is not worth candying less than 6 oranges or lemons or 4 grapefruit, or a mixture, at a time.

Scrub the fruit thoroughly, then cut in half and remove the pulp. Cut the peel into strips and put in a saucepan with enough cold water to cover. Bring to a boil, then cover and simmer 1 to 2 hours, until tender. Change the water two or three times during this period to remove any trace of bitterness, especially if using grapefruit peel.

Drain the peel, reserving the liquid, and put in a heatproof dish. Make up the cooking liquid to 1-1/4 cups with water if necessary and add 1 cup sugar. Heat gently until the sugar has dissolved, then bring to a boil and pour over the peel. Cover with a plate or saucer to keep the peel submerged and leave 2 days.

Pour the syrup back into a saucepan, add 1/2 cup sugar and heat gently until the sugar has dissolved. Bring to a boil, add the peel and simmer gently until it is translucent. Pour back into the dish and leave to soak 2 weeks. At the end of this time, remove the peel from the syrup and place on a wire rack to dry in a warm place two to three days or in a very low oven, no more than 120F (50C), for several hours with the door ajar.

Candied peel contains less sugar than candied fruit; store in an airtight container and use within a few weeks.

Preparing orange, lemon and grapefruit peel for candying

Homemade marrons glacés in box, surrounded by commercially produced ones

Marrons Glacés

It is impossible to reproduce exactly this famous French delicacy at home, but homemade marrons glacés— whole chestnuts candied in vanilla-flavored syrup—have an excellent flavor. They also make stunning decorations for special occasion desserts.

To make marrons glacés you will need 1 pound of fresh sweet chestnuts. Peel and boil chestnuts as described on page 38.

If fresh chestnuts are unavailable, use a 1-1/2 pound can instead. Drain and dry well before using; canned chestnuts do not need boiling first.

Put 2 cups granulated sugar and 1 pound powdered glucose in a large saucepan and heat gently, stirring until both the sugar and glucose have dissolved. Add the chestnuts and bring to a boil. Remove from the heat, transfer to a dish and cover the chestnuts with a plate or saucer to keep them submerged. Leave in a warm place 24 hours. Return the chestnuts to the pan, bring back to a boil, then return to the dish, cover again and leave 24 hours.

On the third day, add 6 to 8 drops vanilla extract and bring to a boil. Cool slightly, then remove the chestnuts with a slotted spoon and put on a wire rack over a plate to dry two to three days.

To give them a glacé finish, prepare syrup and proceed as for candied fruit (page 28), dipping chestnuts in boiling water, then into syrup. Dry on a wire rack in a warm place two to three days or in a very low oven (120F/50C) several hours.

If storing the marrons glacés for any length of time, wrap in foil to prevent hardening.

Nuts

The term "nut" is used to describe any seed or fruit which has an edible kernel encased in a hard or brittle shell. To release the nut kernel, the shell must be cracked open.

For thousands of years nuts were the staple diet of many nomadic tribes. They were popular with the ancient Greeks and Romans too. Rich in protein, vitamins and minerals, nuts still play an invaluable part in the diet, particularly for vegetarians as they can provide much of the protein generally supplied by meat.

Nuts are an excellent source of the B vitamins, vitamin E and various minerals—particularly iron, calcium, phosphorus, magnesium and potassium. Nuts have a high fat content, but much of it is made up of the polyunsaturated and monounsaturated fat, which do not increase blood cholesterol levels. The exception is the coconut, which has a relatively high proportion of saturated fat.

Buying & Storing Nuts

Nuts are available in many forms—shelled and unshelled, sliced, slivered, ground, and also in the form of flour.

Because of their high fat content nuts go rancid if stored for too long, so buy from a store with a good turnover so that the nuts are as fresh as possible.

Nuts in their shells should feel heavy for their size and not rattle around too much—if they rattle it means they have shrivelled. Look for shells with a good uniform color and avoid any that have cracks or holes. If buying shelled nuts, look for plump nuts with a good color.

Nuts in the shell will keep for several months if stored in a cool dry place. (In warmer countries, store in the refrigerator during summer months.) Most shelled nuts will keep 1 to 2 months stored out of direct sunlight in airtight containers.

Using Nuts

Nuts are extremely versatile: they can be used whole as a snack; chopped or ground in sweet recipes, such as cakes, pastries, desserts, cookies, quick breads, crumble toppings, muesli and trail mixes; or in savory dishes like soups, sauces, nut loaves, casseroles and salads. Peanut butter is famous the world over, but other nuts make equally good nut butters; almond, hazelnut and cashew butters are all delicious.

Nut Butters

To make nut butter, put 4 to 6 ounces roasted nuts in a blender or food processor fitted with the metal blade and process until the chopped nuts start to hold together. Add 1 tablespoon sunflower, peanut or sesame oil and continue processing until the mixture reaches the required consistency—chunky or smooth. Store in the refrigerator up to 2 to 3 months.

Chopped & Ground Nuts

Many recipes call for chopped nuts, and the best flavor comes from those freshly chopped. The quickest way is to put the nuts in a blender or food processor fitted with the metal blade and process in short bursts until they are in small neat pieces. A blender or food processor is equally valuable for grinding nuts.

Roasted Nuts

Roasting nuts enhances their flavor and, as it only takes a few minutes, is well worth the effort. Spread the shelled (and skinned, if required) nuts on a baking sheet and roast in the oven at 350F (175C) 10 to 12 minutes until golden.

Toasted Nuts

As a quick alternative to roasting, nuts can be browned under a preheated moderate broiler 2 to 3 minutes, turning frequently. To toast chopped or ground nuts, spread them out in the broiler pan and broil 1 to 2 minutes, turning very frequently, until evenly browned.

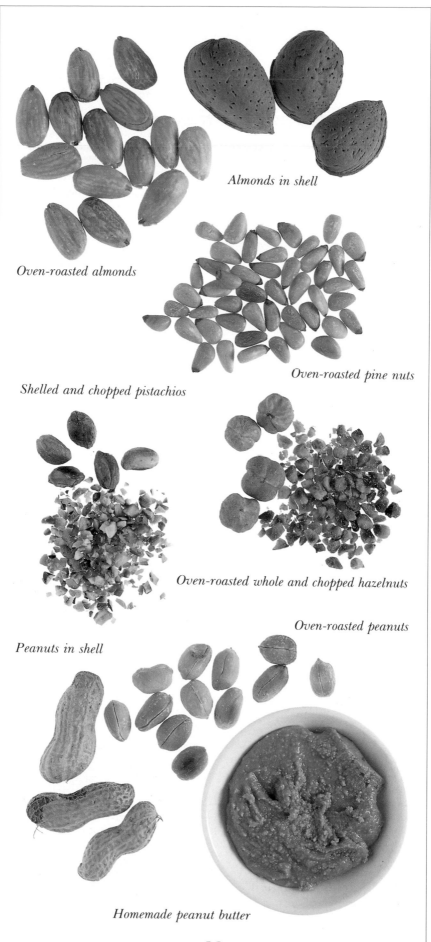

Almonds in shell

Oven-roasted almonds

Oven-roasted pine nuts

Shelled and chopped pistachios

Oven-roasted whole and chopped hazelnuts

Oven-roasted peanuts

Peanuts in shell

Homemade peanut butter

Almond

The almond (*Prunus dulcis*) has been the source of many myths and tales of folklore. Almonds were once held in such esteem that even to dream of them was believed to bring good luck. Almond trees are native to the Middle East, where their beautiful blossoms herald the arrival of spring.

There are two types of almond: sweet and bitter. Sweet almonds are used in a great variety of dishes, particularly in European and Eastern cookery. Bitter almonds are shorter and broader than the sweet variety and owe their bitter flavor to the presence of prussic acid, a toxic substance which can only be removed by heating—they are therefore not eaten raw. Their main use is the production of almond oil and almond extract.

Almonds are rich in calcium, protein and riboflavin. Most of their fat is monounsaturated; their saturated fat level is one of the lowest among nuts.

Almonds are sold unshelled, shelled, blanched with the brown skin removed, chopped, slivered, sliced, roasted and ground. For the best flavor, buy shelled almonds; blanch and remove their skins just before using.

Preparation

To blanch almonds, place the nuts in a pan of cold water, bring to a boil and boil 2 minutes. Drain, then squeeze the nuts out of their skins between finger and thumb.

To toast whole, sliced or ground almonds, spread them out in a broiler pan and place under a moderate broiler 1 to 2 minutes, stirring frequently. Alternatively, brown them in a dry nonstick skillet.

Uses

Almonds make an irresistible snack as they are, or salted or spiced: toast under the broiler, then fry in a little oil until golden. Drain and sprinkle with salt or spices.

Add whole or chopped almonds to cakes, puddings and cookies, breakfast cereals and fruit salads, as well as to stir-fried vegetables or noodles, meat, fish and rice dishes, stuffings, sauces, salads and dips. Almonds make an attractive garnish for vegetable dishes and soups; they are also used as decorations for cakes and cookies.

Ground almonds can be used to replace some of the flour in cakes, giving a lovely moist texture.

Almonds make a very tasty butter (see page 32) or flavored milk, which can be used instead of cow's milk in delicate soups and other dishes. To make almond milk, process 2 to 4 tablespoons blanched almonds in a blender or food processor fitted with the metal blade until finely ground. Add 1 cup warm water, depending on thickness required; process 1 minute. Strain through a double layer of cheesecloth, if wished.

Brazil Nut

The Brazil nut (*Bertholletia excelsa*) is the fruit of the mammoth Brazil tree, which is native to the tropical regions of South America. The trees produce large coconut-type shells inside which the nuts are wedge-like segments.

The fat content of Brazil nuts is one of the highest among nuts, and they have more saturated fat than most other nuts. They also contain several B vitamins and minerals.

Brazil nuts are sold unshelled, shelled, chopped and roasted but they are most often sold shelled, except at Christmas. Their high fat content means they go rancid easily, so buy in small quantities.

Uses

Add Brazil nuts to stir-fried dishes, stuffings, nut loaves and salads. Use in cakes and cookies or add to muesli. Mix ground Brazil nuts with bread crumbs to make a delicious topping or stuffing for vegetables. Whole Brazil nuts can be salted and spiced as for almonds (see above).

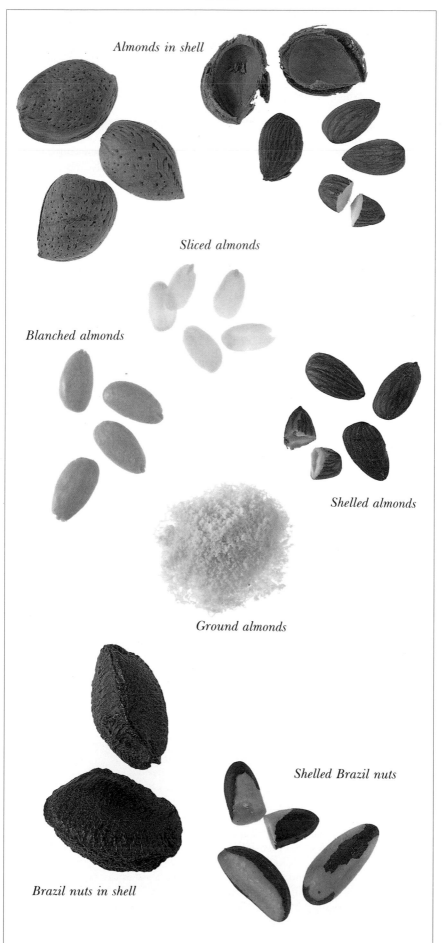

Almonds in shell

Sliced almonds

Blanched almonds

Shelled almonds

Ground almonds

Shelled Brazil nuts

Brazil nuts in shell

Walnut

The walnut (*Juglans regia*) is attributed with certain magical properties, including the ability to ward off disease and make couples fertile— hence the old custom of scattering walnuts at weddings!

Although there are many varieties, there are two main types: the European walnut and the black walnut. European walnuts, which have a sweet yet slightly bitter taste, are also known as English or Persian walnuts. Persian in origin, these walnuts became established in Europe and were introduced into the United States by Spanish missionaries in the 18th century—California is now a major supplier.

Black walnuts are not widely available. They have hard shells and sticky husks which make them far more difficult to process commercially. Their distinctive flavor is stronger than that of the European walnut.

Walnuts have a high fat content but little of it is saturated fat. They provide modest amounts of calcium, iron, phosphorus, potassium and some of the B vitamins.

Walnuts are available shelled or unshelled, chopped and ground. They are also made into a distinctive, nutty-flavored oil—one of the most popular oils for salads—and walnut flour (available mostly from health food shops).

If you have a walnut tree in your garden, pick unripe nuts in early summer—while they are still green and soft enough to pierce right through the shell with a needle. Pickle these in vinegar for serving with cold meats or cheese. Pickled walnuts can also be bought.

Uses
Walnuts add flavor to yeast breads, quick breads, cakes and cookies; use as a decorative topping, too.

Add chopped walnuts to salads, stir-fried vegetables, nut loaves and meatballs. Add ground walnuts to stuffings, or mix with bread crumbs to make savory crumble toppings for casseroles.

Butternut

The butternut (*Juglans cinera*) is a native American nut, also known as white walnut, which grows in New England, especially Vermont. Butternuts are not widely cultivated because it is extremely difficult to shell them and their high proportion of oil makes them go rancid very quickly.

Butternuts are best kept in the refrigerator in hot weather and used within a month. The shells have to be cracked with a hammer in order to remove the nuts. They can be used in the same way as walnuts (see above), in cakes and desserts. They are traditionally used to make maple nut frosting in Vermont.

Pecan

The pecan (*Carya illinoensis*) is the all-American nut. Once the staple food of the American Indians, pecans are now used for such traditional dishes as pecan pie and pecan ice cream.

Pecans grow on tall trees that are a species of hickory and are sometimes referred to as hickory nuts. They resemble walnuts, although the pecan shell is smaller and smooth and their flavor is milder and less bitter.

Pecans are slightly less fatty than walnuts and contain useful minerals and some of the B vitamins.

They are available unshelled, shelled, roasted and chopped.

Uses
Pecans do not need to be blanched or skinned and can be used whole, chopped or ground. They are interchangeable with walnuts in most recipes: use in salads, stuffings, cakes, cookies and candies.

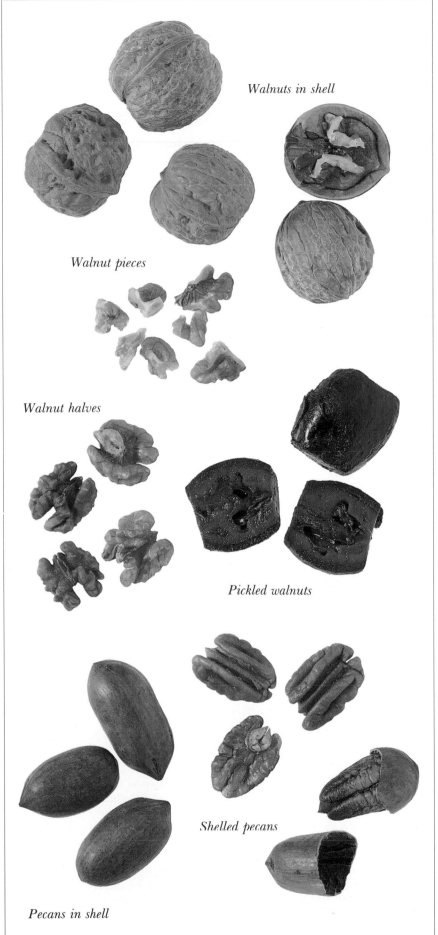

Walnuts in shell

Walnut pieces

Walnut halves

Pickled walnuts

Shelled pecans

Pecans in shell

Chestnut

The chestnut (*Castanea sativa*) is the fruit of the sweet chestnut tree which grows mainly in European countries. Chestnuts should not be confused with horse chestnuts, which are inedible. Chestnuts are sweet and soft, unlike the usual crunchy texture of nuts. The generic name *Castanea* originates from the town Castanis in Thessaly where chestnut trees grow in abundance.

Chestnuts grow in groups of two or three in a prickly green husk. The species containing only a single nut is called *marron*. In parts of southern Europe, chestnuts are used like a vegetable. Chestnut flour is made from ground dried chestnuts.

Chestnuts are sold in their skins, dried, cooked and canned, or as a sweetened or unsweetened puree made from peeled, cooked chestnuts which are pureed—sometimes with cream or vanilla—and sold in cans or tubes.

Chestnuts are low in protein and fat, but rich in carbohydrates. They contain vitamin E, some of the B vitamins and potassium.

Fresh chestnuts will only keep at room temperature for a short time. They can, however, be stored in the refrigerator two to three months.

Preparation

Both the outer and inner skins have to be removed and the nuts cooked—either by roasting or boiling—before they can be eaten.

To peel chestnuts, make a slit in the skin near the pointed end, then put in a saucepan, cover with boiling water and leave 2 to 3 minutes. Remove from the water one at a time and peel off the thick, dark outer skin and the thin inner skin. Chestnuts are much easier to peel while still warm. Boil again if skins are difficult to remove. If the chestnuts are to be roasted, leave the thin inner skin on.

To roast chestnuts, bake in the oven at 400F (205C) 20 minutes, then peel off the inner skin. Or roast over an open fire.

To boil chestnuts, put them in a saucepan, cover with a mixture of half milk and half water, cover and simmer gently 20 to 30 minutes, or until soft. Drain and sieve if a puree is required. One pound fresh chestnuts will yield 12 ounces peeled ones, which will in turn yield 14 ounces boiled chestnuts—as they absorb some of the cooking liquid.

Dried chestnuts should be soaked in hot water 30 to 60 minutes or in cold water overnight, then cooked as for fresh chestnuts.

Uses

The rich flavor of chestnuts goes well in both savory and sweet dishes. They make a rich, full-flavored stuffing, especially good for the traditional Christmas turkey. Chestnuts also make a delicious soup, or they can be added to vegetables such as Brussels sprouts. In France, chestnuts are used in all manner of elegant desserts and cakes.

Large whole chestnuts can be candied to make the French delicacy marrons glacés (see page 31).

Chestnut flour can be used to make cakes and fritters; use in equal quantities with all-purpose flour.

Beechnut

The beechnut (*Fagus sylvatica* of the beech tree is a small, three-sided dark brown nut enclosed in a prickly husk. Beechnuts can be gathered as they fall, in the autumn. Beech trees do not produce an abundant crop each year; they may only have a bumper crop every five or eight years. Beechnuts are not usually sold in the shops.

The flavor of the beechnut is between that of the hazelnut and chestnut. The slightly bitter flavor disappears when these nuts are roasted. They can be peeled and roasted like chestnuts (see above), but as they are very small, they are rather time consuming to peel. Beechnuts are best eaten on their own or used in stuffings.

Chestnut in husk

Whole chestnuts

Peeled and skinned chestnuts

Dried chestnuts

Boiled chestnuts

Chestnut purée

Coconut

The coconut (*Cocos nucifera*) is the fruit of a palm tree which grows in the South Sea and Pacific Islands, and in Southeast Asia. Coconuts are at their best when freshly picked and young, with greenish white skins; they are rarely available in this form outside their country of origin.

The coconut has a delicious and nutritious milky liquid and flesh. It also provides an oil—extracted from the dried flesh. Even the sap from the tree is used—it is fermented to produce arrack. Coconut flesh or "meat" can be eaten as it is; compressed into blocks, known as coconut cream; or dried.

The dried flesh is sold as flaked or shredded coconut—flakes being the largest pieces and shredded the smallest. Most flaked and shredded coconut is sold in packages mixed with sugar. Opened packages of dried coconut can be stored in the refrigerator for several months, or in an airtight jar for a few weeks. Dried coconut freezes very successfully and can be stored for months in the freezer.

If buying a fresh coconut, look for one that feels heavy when you pick it up; you should also be able to hear the liquid moving around inside when you shake it. Coconuts travel a long way to reach the markets and sometimes the liquid inside has dried up by the time they reach their destination. Make sure that the three pores or bald patches on the shell known as "eyes" are dry with no sign of mold and no rancid smell. Coconut flesh can be kept in the refrigerator up to a week.

The liquid inside the coconut is often referred to as milk, but this is slightly misleading; when recipes call for coconut milk they do not mean the liquid from the coconut but milk made by steeping coconut flesh or creamed coconut in water (see below). Coconut liquid can be kept, covered, in the refrigerator for up to 2 days.

Coconut has a very high fat content, nearly all of which is saturated fat. Coconut oil therefore has a high saturated fat level, unlike other vegetable and nut oils. Coconut contains some of the B vitamins and useful minerals.

Preparation

To open a coconut, pierce the eyes with a hammer and screwdriver and drain the liquid into a cup. Crack the shell by hitting the widest part of the coconut all the way around with a hammer. Separate the halves and cut the flesh away from the shell with a sharp knife. Cut into chunks or grate to use.

Freshly grated or shredded coconut can be toasted in the oven at 350F (175C) until golden, or spread in a broiler pan and toasted under a very low heat, shaking frequently.

Uses

As well as making a delicious drink, the coconut liquid can be added to spicy vegetable mixtures and curry sauces. Coconut milk (see below) can also be used in curries, rice dishes and desserts. Dried coconut is mainly used in baking, particularly for cakes and cookies, both in the mixture and for toppings and decoration. Toasted coconut makes an attractive garnish for vegetable dishes.

To Make Coconut Milk

Put the freshly grated coconut in a bowl, add 2/3 cup cold water and let stand 15 to 20 minutes. Squeeze the coconut firmly to extract as much liquid as possible, allowing the liquid to fall into a separate bowl. This will yield "thick" coconut milk. Repeat the process, with the same coconut flesh, letting stand 10 to 15 minutes the second time. Squeeze the liquid into a second bowl. This will yield "thin" coconut milk. Mix the two together if required.

To make coconut milk from creamed coconut, cut off a 2 ounce piece and mix with 2/3 cup hot water.

Coconut milk can also be made using dried coconut: put 2-2/3 cups dried coconut in a bowl, pour over 1/2 cup hot water, let stand 1 hour, then squeeze out the liquid.

Halved fresh coconut

Grated fresh coconut

Dried coconut

Flaked dried coconut

Creamed coconut

Peanut

Peanuts are probably the most widely used nut in the United States and Britain, but are well loved in many other parts of the world as well.

The peanut (*Arachis hypogaea*) is actually a legume—the seed of an annual pod-bearing plant originating in South America—but they are always used like nuts. They grow underground, encased in a dry, fibrous, straw-colored shell—hence their alternative name, groundnut. They are also known as monkey nuts.

Peanuts are highly nutritious; they have a high protein content and also contain some of the B vitamins, vitamin E and minerals.

It is believed that peanuts contain a substance which is believed to interfere with the body's absorption of nutrients. However, this substance is easily destroyed by cooking—and in fact, the flavor of peanuts is much improved by roasting (see page 32).

Peanuts are available shelled or unshelled, skinned, roasted, or roasted and salted. Peanut butter is probably the most famous product made from peanuts; they are also used to make peanut or groundnut oil.

Unshelled peanuts will stay fresh for several months in a cool dry place. Shelled peanuts will keep for 2 months in a cool place, longer in the refrigerator.

Preparation
To remove the skins, put the peanuts in a broiler pan and toast under medium heat, shaking from time to time, until the skins can be removed by rubbing them between the finger and thumb. Put the peanuts in a bag and rub together until all the skins have been removed. Alternatively, bake in a 350F (175C) oven and then rub off the skins.

Uses
More peanuts are probably eaten as a snack than all the other nuts put together, but they do have other uses. As peanuts are cheaper than many other nuts, they are particularly attractive to vegetarians: they can also be used in stews, nut loaves, turnovers and sauces. Use chopped or ground peanuts in cakes and cookies. Salt or spice them the same way as almonds (see page 34).

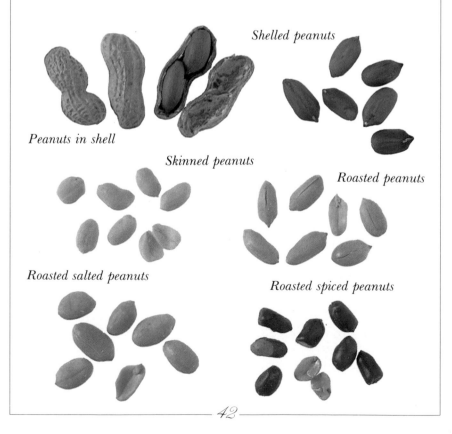

Shelled peanuts

Peanuts in shell

Skinned peanuts

Roasted peanuts

Roasted salted peanuts

Roasted spiced peanuts

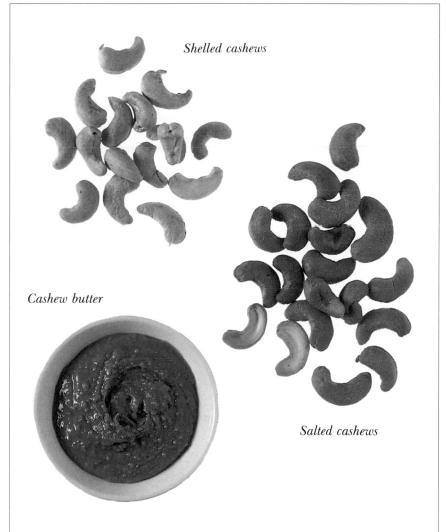

Shelled cashews

Cashew butter

Salted cashews

Cashew

Cashew nuts (*Anacardium occidentale*) are found hanging at the base of the small, pear-shaped, reddish fruit of the cashew tree, which originated in Brazil. The fruit, known as a cashew apple, is sometimes eaten in preference to the nuts. The nuts have a fairly soft texture and a subtle flavor.

Cashew nuts have two layers of shell; in between is a caustic substance called *cardol* which can cause blisters and irritation if it comes in contact with the skin. To prevent any danger of this, the nuts are always roasted and shelled, then heated again to remove the inner layer before they are sold. They may also be roasted and salted.

Cashew nuts contain some of the B group vitamins, vitamin A, calcium and iron.

Uses
They are usually eaten as a snack—salted cashews are especially popular for serving with drinks. To salt cashews, fry in oil until browned all over, drain on paper towels, then sprinkle with salt.

Cashews are frequently used in stir-fried Chinese dishes. Toasted cashews are delicious sprinkled on salads, cooked vegetables and fruit. Toast them under the broiler or in a dry nonstick skillet as for almonds (see page 34).

Use chopped or ground cashews in stuffings, nut loaves, meatballs and sauces. As they go soft when baked in a wet mixture, cashews are not usually added to cake mixtures, but can be used in drier cookie mixtures. They can also be made into nut butter (see page 32).

Hazelnut

The hazelnut (*Corylus avellana*), filbert and cob nut all belong to the hazel family. There is little difference between them and they are interchangeable in recipes.

Originally cultivated in the Mediterranean area, hazelnuts are now grown in Turkey and many parts of Europe. The nuts, which grow in clusters, are partially covered by a green skin, rather like a hat. They are rich in vitamin E and some of the B vitamins.

Hazelnuts are available unshelled, shelled, roasted, chopped and ground. Shelled nuts need to be skinned for use in cakes or desserts or to make nut butter. (Skin the same way as peanuts, see page 42.) Whole, ground or chopped hazelnuts can also be toasted (see page 32).

Uses

Hazelnuts are used in cakes, pastries and desserts. They are famed for their use in pies and their affinity with chocolate. Hazelnuts are popular with vegetarians for their inclusion in nut loaves and nut bread; they also make delicious nut butter (see page 32).

Pine Nut

Pine nuts (*Pinus pinea*) are the edible seeds of a number of pine trees, mainly the stone pine, which are native to the Mediterranean. They are also known as pine kernels, pignolas and Indian nuts. The tiny nuts are cream-colored and have a rich, tangy pine flavor. They grow in a soft shell and have no skin.

A different variety, the pinon, from the pinon tree is used in American Indian and Mexican cooking, and is available in the American Southwest.

Pine nuts are more expensive than most other nuts but their strong flavor ensures that a small amount goes a long way.

Oils present in pine nuts go rancid very quickly, so store the nuts in a cool place—in the refrigerator in hot weather. Pine nuts are available raw, roasted and salted; they can be used whole or chopped. Their resinous flavor mellows if the nuts are toasted (see page 32).

Uses

Pine nuts can be eaten raw like peanuts, or used in soups, salads, rice dishes, stews, stuffings and sauces. In Italy they are used to make the famous pesto sauce served with pasta. They are also used in Middle Eastern dishes, such as stuffed vine leaves, and in Greek pastries and cakes.

Tiger Nut

The tiger nut (*Cyperus esculentus sativus*) is a small, brown, knobby nut with a flavor similar to that of the almond. Tiger nuts are not in fact true nuts but are the rhizomes of a plant native to Africa. They are also known as earth almonds or chufa nuts.

Tiger nuts are available whole or ground. The older, more shrivelled ones have a sweeter taste than the fresh looking ones. They will store indefinitely in an airtight container in a cool place.

Uses

Tiger nuts can be eaten raw or roasted as a snack, or added to stuffings, cakes, desserts and sweets.

They are also used to make the Spanish drink *horchata de chufa*. Lightly toast 1 pound tiger nuts, then soak 2 to 3 hours in 2-1/2 cups water with sugar and cinnamon to taste. Puree in a blender or food processor fitted with the metal blade, let stand for a few hours, then strain through cheesecloth. The result is a delicately flavored milk.

Shelled hazelnuts

Hazelnuts in shell

Roasted hazelnuts

Roasted chopped hazelnuts

Roasted ground hazelnuts

Hazelnut butter

Pine nuts

Tiger nuts

Pistachio

The pistachio nut (*Pistacia vera*) is revered in the Middle East and India for its attractive green color and exquisite flavor. The pistachio tree is native to central and western Asia.

Pistachios are usually sold in their opened shells and can be removed quite easily by prying the shells apart. They can be eaten with the skins on, but if you want the delicate green color the skins must be removed.

Preparation

To remove the skins, put the nuts in a broiler pan and toast under a medium heat, shaking from time to time, until the skins can be removed easily by rubbing them between your finger and thumb. Put the nuts in a bag and rub together until all the skins are removed. Alternatively, bake them in a 350F (175C) oven and then rub off the skins.

Pistachios contain vitamin A, some B vitamins and minerals.

Uses

Their attractive color makes pistachios a favorite for decorating desserts and cakes, and for adding a splash of color to savory recipes, especially pâtés and terrines. They can be chopped and used to give flavor to stuffings, nut loaves, meatballs and spiced rice. Pistachios are also served as a delicious snack, in or out of their shells.

Macadamia

The macadamia (*Macadamia ternifolia*) is a large round nut native to Australia but also cultivated in Hawaii. Macadamias are sometimes known as Queensland nuts. Their firm texture and sweet flavor make them a prized delicacy.

Macadamias have a very hard shell that is difficult to crack and, because they have a tendency to become mildewed in the shell, they are usually sold shelled, either raw or roasted. They are generally sold whole, although they may also be available in pieces.

Macadamias contain minerals plus several B vitamins. Like Brazil nuts, they have a high fat content and go rancid quite quickly, so use soon after purchase.

Uses

Macadamias are mainly eaten on their own as a snack, either plain or salted, but they can be used in desserts and cakes. They add a pleasant texture and flavor to stir-fried vegetable and seafood dishes.

Ginkgo Nut

The yellowy-colored ginkgo nut is a traditional food at Japanese weddings. It is also known as *jingko*, *bok gwa*, *pai kuo* and *ginnan*.

Ginkgo nuts are sold fresh in Japan and China and sometimes in the United States but are not widely available elsewhere. They are available canned in brine, but usually only from ethnic stores.

Preparation

Fresh ginkgo nuts must be shelled and cooked before eating. To shell, pour boiling water over the nuts and soak 5 to 10 minutes. Drain, cool, then peel off the skins. The nuts can then be stir-fried, roasted or deep-fried.

Canned ginkgo nuts can be drained and stored in the refrigerator in a covered jar of water up to 2 weeks; change the water every other day. Shelled, blanched nuts can be stored the same way.

Uses

Ginkgo nuts are prized for their meaty flavor and are used mainly as a garnish for soups and vegetable dishes—they turn bright green as they cook.

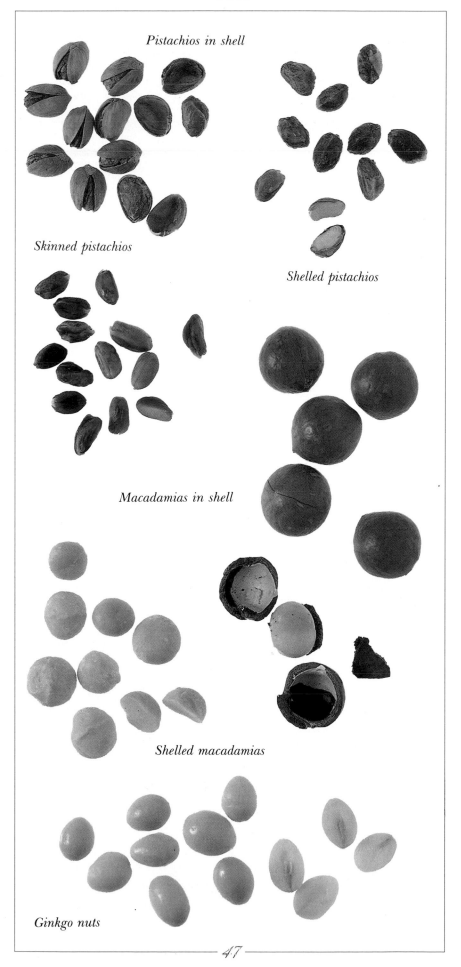

Pistachios in shell

Skinned pistachios

Shelled pistachios

Macadamias in shell

Shelled macadamias

Ginkgo nuts

Tarator Soup

2/3 cup walnut pieces
2 garlic cloves
2 tablespoons olive oil
1-1/4 cups milk
1-1/4 cups plain yogurt
Salt and pepper, to taste
1/4 cucumber
TO GARNISH:
Dill sprigs

1. Put walnuts and garlic in a food processor fitted with the metal blade and process until finely chopped.
2. With motor running, gradually add oil through the feed tube until a smooth puree forms. Pour in milk and process until smooth. Put yogurt in a large bowl. Gradually pour in blended mixture, stirring until thoroughly mixed. Season with salt and pepper to taste.
3. Peel and chop cucumber; stir into soup and refrigerate 2 hours. Pour into individual soup bowls and garnish with dill.

Makes 4 servings.

Variation: Replace walnut pieces with hazelnuts.

Cashew & Fennel Soup

4 white bread slices, crusts removed
2/3 cup water
1 cup cashews
1 to 2 garlic cloves
3 tablespoons lemon juice
1-3/4 cups milk
Salt and pepper, to taste
2 tablespoons chopped fennel
CROÛTONS:
2 white bread slices, crusts removed
Vegetable oil

1. Put bread in a medium-size bowl and add 2/3 cup water; let soften 5 minutes. Put cashews in a food processor fitted with the metal blade and chop finely. Add soaked bread and water, garlic to taste, lemon juice, 3/4 cup milk and seasoning; process until smooth, then turn into a bowl.
2. Stir in remaining milk and fennel, cover and refrigerate 1 hour.

3. To make croûtons, cut bread into 1/4-inch cubes. Heat oil in a small skillet and fry bread, turning occasionally, until pale golden-brown. Remove with a slotted spoon and drain on paper towels. Pour soup into individual soup bowls and sprinkle with croûtons to serve.

Makes 4 servings.

Chestnut & Madeira Soup

2 carrots
1 onion
2 celery stalks
1 tablespoon vegetable oil
1 tablespoon all-purpose flour
3 cups vegetable or chicken stock
1 bouquet garni
2 chervil sprigs
Salt and pepper, to taste
1 pound peeled, cooked chestnuts, sieved (see page 38)
2/3 cup half and half
1/3 cup medium-dry sherry
TO SERVE:
3 tablespoons half and half
Chervil sprigs
Croûtons (see page 49)

1. Dice the carrots, onion and celery. In a medium-size saucepan, heat oil and cook onion until softened. Stir in flour, then add celery, carrots, stock, bouquet garni, chervil and seasoning. Bring to a boil, stirring, then cover, reduce heat and simmer gently 20 minutes, until vegetables are tender.
2. Remove bouquet garni. Pour into a blender or food processor fitted with the metal blade and process until smooth; return half to saucepan. Add sieved chestnuts and half and half to remaining soup in blender or food processor and process until smooth.

3. Pour into the saucepan with sherry and simmer 5 minutes, until heated through. Pour into individual soup bowls and swirl a little half and half into each one. Garnish with chervil and serve with croûtons.

Makes 6 servings.

Note: A 15-1/2-ounce can unsweetened chestnut puree can be used instead of fresh chestnuts.

Bouquet garni: 1 sprig each of thyme and parsley and 1 bay leaf tied in cheesecloth.

Cashew & Blue Cheese Dip

2 ounces cashews
6 chervil sprigs
2 ounces blue cheese
3 ounces fromage frais or plain yogurt
Salt and pepper, to taste
Milk (optional)
CRUDITÉS:
6 quail eggs
1 head Belgian endive
2 ounces snow peas
2 ounces baby carrots
1/2 fennel bulb
1 bunch of radishes
4 ounces cherry tomatoes
1 red apple, quartered and cored
1 teaspoon lemon juice

1. Put nuts and chervil in a food processor fitted with the metal blade and chop finely. Add cheese, fromage frais and seasoning and process to a puree, adding a little milk if necessary. Turn into a serving bowl.

2. To prepare crudités, boil quail eggs 2 minutes, put into cold water, remove when cool and shell.

3. Prepare vegetables: divide Belgian endive into leaves; remove ends and any strings from snow peas; peel carrots; cut fennel into thin wedges; leave tops on radishes and tomatoes. Slice apple and brush with lemon juice to prevent discoloration. Place the bowl of dip in the center of a large serving dish; arrange crudités around dip.

Makes 4 to 6 servings.

Variation: Use almonds or hazelnuts instead of cashews if you prefer.

Walnut, Stilton & Pear Salad

2 ripe pears
1/4 head chicory
Few radicchio leaves
Handful of arugula leaves
4 ounces Stilton cheese, cut into cubes
1/2 cup chopped walnuts
MELBA TOAST:
4 thin slices white bread
DRESSING:
2 tablespoons walnut oil
2 teaspoons cider vinegar
Salt and pepper, to taste

1. First make Melba toast: preheat oven to 350F (175C). Toast bread, then remove crusts. Slice toast in half horizontally and place toasted side down on a baking sheet. Bake in the oven 5 minutes, until curled.

For the dressing: put all ingredients in a jar with a lid and shake thoroughly until well mixed; pour into a bowl.

2. Quarter pears, remove cores and slice into dressing; mix gently to coat with dressing, which will prevent them from discoloring.

3. Break chicory and radicchio into bite-size pieces and add to bowl with arugula leaves, Stilton and walnuts; toss thoroughly. Serve on individual plates with Melba toast.

Makes 4 servings.

Note: If arugula is unavailable, substitute a few lettuce leaves.

Avocado & Grapefruit Salad

2 pink grapefruit
1 large avocado, halved and pitted
1 teaspoon lemon juice
WALNUT SAUCE:
2/3 cup walnut pieces
1 tablespoon walnut oil
1 teaspoon lemon juice
1/4 cup plain yogurt
Salt and pepper, to taste
TO GARNISH:
Dill sprigs

1. Peel grapefruit with a serrated knife and cut into sections, removing all pith and membrane.

2. Peel each avocado half and slice lengthwise; brush with lemon juice to prevent discoloration. Arrange alternate, overlapping slices of avocado and grapefruit on 4 individual serving plates.

3. To make sauce, place all ingredients in a blender or food processor fitted with the metal blade and process until smooth; turn into a bowl. Spoon a little sauce on the side of each plate. Garnish with dill and serve accompanied by Melba toast (see opposite).

Makes 4 servings.

Mediterranean Pine Nut Salad

2 eggplants, sliced
Salt
6 tablespoons virgin olive oil
2 garlic cloves, chopped
1 red bell pepper, seeded and sliced into rings
4 large tomatoes, peeled and chopped
2 tablespoons chopped parsley
Pepper, to taste
TO GARNISH:
Thinly sliced onion rings
1/4 cup pine nuts, toasted
1 tablespoon chopped parsley
6 ripe olives, halved and pitted

1. Put eggplants in a colander, sprinkle with salt and leave 30 minutes. Rinse well and pat dry with paper towels. This will rid them of their bitter juices, and prevent them from absorbing too much oil during frying.
2. In a large skillet, heat a little oil and fry eggplant slices in batches until golden on both sides, adding more oil as necessary. Drain on paper towels.

3. Heat a little more oil in the pan, add garlic and bell pepper and cook 1 minute. Add tomatoes, parsley and fried eggplant, season with salt and pepper, cover and simmer 10 minutes, stirring occasionally. Turn into a shallow serving dish, arrange onion rings on top, then sprinkle with pine nuts, parsley and olives.

Makes 6 servings.

Tomato Salad with Pesto

1 pound tomatoes
2 tablespoons ripe olives, halved and pitted
3 ounces Feta cheese, crumbled
PESTO VINAIGRETTE:
2 tablespoons each chopped fresh basil and parsley
1 small garlic clove, crushed
1/4 cup pine nuts
2 tablespoons grated Parmesan cheese
2 tablespoons lemon juice
1/3 cup olive oil
Pepper, to taste
HERB LOAF:
1 French bread loaf
1/4 cup butter, softened
3 tablespoons chopped mixed herbs (parsley, chives,
thyme, marjoram)
Salt and pepper, to taste

1. First make vinaigrette: put herbs, garlic, pine nuts and Parmesan cheese in a food processor fitted with the metal blade and chop finely. With the motor running, gradually pour in lemon juice and oil through the feed tube; add pepper, to taste.

2. Slice tomatoes and arrange in 6 individual serving dishes. Pour vinaigrette over tomatoes. Sprinkle olives and cheese over the top and let stand 1 hour before serving, for the flavors to mingle.

3. To make herb loaf, preheat oven to 400F (205C). Slice bread diagonally, but not quite all the way through. Cream butter with herbs and seasoning; spread some on each side of every cut. Wrap in foil and bake 15 minutes; loosen foil at the top and bake 5 minutes, to crisp. Slice and serve hot with the tomato salad.

Makes 6 servings.

Scallop & Asparagus Croustades

1 (8- to 9-inch) unsliced sandwich loaf
3 tablespoons sunflower oil
FILLING:
4 ounces asparagus
6 scallops, cleaned
1/2 cup white wine
Bouquet garni (see page 50)
1 small onion, chopped
4 ounces button mushrooms, sliced
1 tablespoon plus 1 teaspoon all-purpose flour
3 tablespoons whipping cream
1 ounce pine nuts, toasted

1. Preheat oven to 400F (205C). Cut 6 (1-1/4-inch) slices from the loaf; cut into 3-inch squares. Cut out the center, leaving a bottom and a 1/4-inch border. Brush all over with 2 tablespoons oil, place on a baking sheet and bake in the oven 10 minutes, until crisp and golden.

2. Meanwhile, for the filling, cut asparagus into 1-1/2-inch lengths. Cook stalks in boiling water 5 minutes; add tips and cook 3 minutes. Drain, reserving 1/4 cup liquid. Cut each scallop into 4 pieces.

Put wine, reserved liquid and bouquet garni in a saucepan and bring to a boil. Add scallops, cover and cook gently 3 minutes; remove with a slotted spoon. Boil cooking liquid until reduced to 2/3 cup.

3. In a pan, heat remaining oil and fry onion until softened; add mushrooms and cook 2 minutes. Remove from heat, stir in flour, then gradually stir in reduced liquid. Bring to a boil and cook, stirring, 2 minutes, until thickened. Add cream; return scallops and asparagus to pan with pine nuts and heat through. Spoon into warmed croustades and serve.

Makes 6 servings.

Asparagus & Nut Dressing

1 pound asparagus
Salt
MACADAMIA DRESSING:
2 ounces macadamia nuts
6 large chervil sprigs
1/4 cup hazelnut oil
1 tablespoon lemon juice
1/4 teaspoon honey
Salt and pepper, to taste

1. Bend lower end of asparagus so that it snaps—it will do this naturally at the point where it becomes tough. Tie asparagus in a bundle and put upright in an asparagus steamer or tall saucepan, with sufficient boiling salted water to come 2 inches up stems.

2. Cover, making a lid with foil and doming it over asparagus tips if necessary, so that the heads cook in steam. Simmer until tender: 15 minutes for small asparagus, 20 to 30 minutes for thicker stems. Lift asparagus from pan, drain very carefully and arrange on a serving platter.

3. To make dressing, place nuts and all but 1 small sprig of chervil in a blender or food processor fitted with the metal blade; chop finely. Add remaining ingredients and process until smooth. Spoon dressing over asparagus and garnish with remaining chervil.

Makes 4 servings.

Gruyère & Walnut Tartlets

PASTRY:
1-1/4 cups all-purpose flour
6 tablespoons butter, chilled
1/3 cup walnut pieces, ground
1 to 2 tablespoons ice water
FILLING:
6 ounces asparagus
2 eggs
2 ounces cream cheese
2/3 cup half and half
1 cup shredded Gruyère cheese (4 oz.)
1/2 cup chopped walnuts
1 tablespoon chopped fresh tarragon
Salt and pepper, to taste
TO GARNISH:
Salad leaves

1. To make pastry, sift flour into a bowl. Cut in butter until mixture resembles bread crumbs. Add ground walnuts and 1 to 2 tablespoons ice water, mixing to a smooth firm dough. On a lightly floured surface, knead lightly, then wrap in plastic wrap and refrigerate 15 minutes. Roll out pastry thinly and divide into 6 pieces. Roll into circles and use to line 6 (3-1/2-inch) individual flan pans; prick the bottoms. Refrigerate 15 minutes. Preheat oven to 400F (205C).

2. To make filling, cut asparagus into 1/2-inch lengths, cook in boiling water 5 minutes, then drain. In a medium-size bowl, mix eggs and cottage cheese together until smooth; add half and half, cheese, chopped walnuts, asparagus, tarragon and seasoning.
3. Spoon into pastry shells and bake 25 minutes, until puffed and set. Garnish with salad leaves to serve.

Makes 6 servings.

Goat Cheese & Walnut Parcels

2 sheets filo pastry
2 tablespoons butter, melted
1 (6-1/2-oz.) roll goat cheese, 1-3/4-inch diameter
2 tablespoons chopped walnuts
6 chives
Vegetable oil for deep-frying
TOMATO SAUCE:
1 tablespoon olive oil
1 small onion, chopped
1 garlic clove, crushed
1 pound tomatoes, peeled, seeded and chopped
2 teaspoons tomato paste
Salt and pepper, to taste
TO GARNISH:
Chervil sprigs

1. Cut filo pastry into 12 (6-inch) squares; pile on top of each other and cover with a clean towel to prevent pastry drying out. Brush 1 pastry square with butter, lay another square on top and brush again with butter.

2. Cut goat cheese into 3/4-inch slices and lay a slice in the center of pastry square; sprinkle with chopped walnuts. Bring up edges of pastry and pinch together into a "money" bag shape—butter will help the pastry to stick. Repeat with remaining pastry, cheese and walnuts. Tie a chive around the top of each.

3. To make sauce, heat oil in a small pan, add onion and fry until softened. Add garlic, tomatoes, tomato paste and seasoning, cover and simmer 10 minutes. Sieve, then reheat.

In a deep pan, heat oil until a cube of bread turns brown in 1 minute. Put 3 parcels in the hot oil and deep-fry 2 minutes, until crisp and golden-brown, turning once. Repeat with remaining parcels.

Serve immediately, accompanied by the sauce and garnished with chervil.

Makes 6 servings.

Turbot with Pine Nuts

1 tablespoon vegetable oil
1 small onion, finely chopped
4 turbot cutlets, about 7 ounces each
1/2 cup white wine
1/4 cup water
Salt and pepper, to taste
1 tablespoon chopped dill
1/4 cup whipping cream
1/4 cup pine nuts, toasted
TO GARNISH:
Dill sprigs

1. In a large skillet, heat oil, add onion and cook until softened. Add fish, pour over wine and 1/4 cup water and sprinkle with salt and pepper. Cover and simmer 5 minutes, until the fish is opaque and just cooked. Remove with a spatula and arrange on a warmed serving dish; reserve cooking liquid.

2. Sieve liquid, pressing through onion. Return to saucepan and boil rapidly to reduce by half, then add dill and cream. Adjust seasoning if necessary.

3. Heat through gently, then pour over fish. Sprinkle with pine nuts and garnish with dill sprigs to serve.

Makes 4 servings.

Shrimp with Cashews

2 tablespoons vegetable oil
3 ounces cashew nuts (2/3 cup)
2 garlic cloves, sliced
1 (1/2-inch) piece gingerroot, peeled and chopped
1 red bell pepper, thinly sliced
4 ounces snow peas, topped and tailed
6 ounces shiitake mushrooms, stalks removed, halved
1 teaspoon cornstarch
1 tablespoon each soy sauce and sherry
12 ounces shrimp, thawed if frozen
4 green onions, sliced diagonally
1/2 teaspoon five-spice powder
6 ounces bean sprouts
1 teaspoon sesame oil
Salt and pepper, to taste

1. In a wok, heat half the oil, add cashews and stir-fry until golden-brown. Remove from wok and set aside.

2. Add remaining oil to wok, then add garlic, gingerroot, bell pepper, snow peas and mushrooms and stir-fry 4 minutes.

3. Blend cornstarch with soy sauce and sherry; add to wok with shrimp. Stir until thickened, then add green onions, five-spice powder, cashews and bean sprouts and stir-fry 1 to 2 minutes, to heat through. Add sesame oil, season with salt and pepper, and serve with cooked rice.

Makes 4 servings.

Circassian Chicken

1 (3-lb.) chicken
1 onion, quartered
1 carrot, quartered
1 celery stalk, sliced
Bouquet garni (see page 50)
SAUCE:
2 white bread slices, crusts removed, chopped
1/4 cup milk
12 ounces walnut pieces (about 2-2/3 cups)
1 teaspoon lemon juice
1 garlic clove, crushed
Salt and pepper, to taste
TO GARNISH:
1 tablespoon walnut oil
1 teaspoon paprika
1 tablespoon chopped fresh parsley

1. Put chicken, onion, carrot, celery and bouquet garni in a large saucepan. Cover with cold water, bring to a boil, then cover and simmer gently about 1 hour, until cooked. Remove chicken from pan; strain stock and reserve. When cool enough to handle, remove chicken flesh from bone, cut into large pieces and keep warm.
2. To make sauce, put bread into a medium-size bowl. Add milk and soak 5 minutes. Put nuts in a food processor fitted with the metal blade and process until finely ground. Add bread and milk, lemon juice, garlic, seasoning and 1-1/4 cups reserved stock; process until smooth and about the consistency of whipping cream. Pour into a saucepan to reheat, adding a little more stock and seasoning if necessary.
3. Arrange chicken on a warmed serving dish and pour over sauce. Mix oil and paprika together and drizzle over the surface, then sprinkle with parsley. Serve warm or cold, with rice.

Makes 4 servings.

Chicken Satay with Peanut Sauce

4 chicken breasts, skinned and boned
MARINADE:
2 tablespoons soy sauce
2 garlic cloves, crushed
1 tablespoon lemon juice
PEANUT SAUCE:
1/3 cup peanuts, toasted and skinned
2 tablespoons vegetable oil
1 small onion, chopped
2 garlic cloves, crushed
1/4 teaspoon chili powder
1 teaspoon ground coriander
1 teaspoon ground cumin
1/3 cup tomato juice
Water
1 teaspoon soy sauce
1 teaspoon lemon juice

1. Mix marinade ingredients together in a medium-size bowl. Cut chicken breasts into 1-inch cubes; add to marinade, stir to coat completely and marinate 2 hours.

2. To make peanut sauce, put peanuts in a food processor fitted with the metal blade and chop finely. In a pan, heat oil, add onion and fry until softened. Add garlic, spices and peanuts and cook 1 minute. Mix in tomato juice, cook 1 minute, then gradually blend in enough water to make a good consistency. Bring to a boil, stirring; cook, stirring, until thickened. Add soy sauce and lemon juice; keep warm.

3. Thread chicken pieces onto 4 skewers. Cook under a preheated hot broiler 4 to 5 minutes on each side, basting frequently with the marinade. Serve with cooked rice and peanut sauce.

Makes 4 servings.

Note: To make green onion flowers for a garnish, trim, then shred the top leaving the bottom intact. Place in iced water to open.

Chicken & Filo Roulade

4 skinned chicken breasts, about 3 ounces each
4 lean smoked ham slices
2/3 cup walnut halves
2 ounces Stilton cheese
2 sheets filo pastry
1 tablespoon butter, melted
SAUCE:
1/3 cup walnut pieces
1 ounce Stilton cheese
1 garlic clove, chopped
1/3 cup half and half
2 tablespoons snipped chives
Salt and pepper, to taste
TO GARNISH:
Salad leaves

1. Slice horizontally three-quarters of the way through chicken breasts; open them out, cover with plastic wrap and beat with a rolling pin to flatten. Cover each with a slice of ham; trim to fit. Chop walnuts in a food processor fitted with the metal blade; add Stilton and blend to a paste. Spread over the ham, roll up loosely like a jellyroll, and set aside. Preheat oven to 375F (190C).

2. Cut filo pastry in half lengthwise to make 4 (13" x 9") rectangles; pile on top of each other and cover with a clean towel to prevent pastry drying out. Take 1 rectangle and brush with butter; put a chicken roulade at the

lower end. Roll up from the short side folding in pastry at sides. Repeat with remaining chicken and pastry. Place on a baking sheet. Brush all over with butter, and bake 30 minutes, until crisp and golden.

3. To make sauce, chop walnuts in a food processor fitted with the metal blade; add Stilton, garlic and half and half and process until smooth. Turn into a small saucepan, add chives and seasoning and heat gently. Serve roulades sliced, on warmed individual plates, with sauce to one side. Garnish with salad leaves.

Makes 4 servings.

Chicken & Asparagus in Baskets

2 sheets filo pastry
6 ounces asparagus tips
2 tablespoons vegetable oil
1 onion, sliced
1 garlic clove, chopped
4 ounces button mushrooms
2 tablespoons all-purpose flour
1 cup chicken stock
1 tablespoon chopped fresh tarragon
2 tablespoons half and half
8 ounces cooked chicken, cut into fingers
1/2 cup pistachios (2 ounces), halved
Salt and pepper, to taste

1. Preheat oven to 375F (190C). Cut filo pastry into 6-inch squares; pile on top of each other and cover with a clean towel to prevent pastry drying out. Drape 3 squares of pastry each over 4 inverted individual 6 ounce bombe molds (or similar ovenproof molds) and place on a baking sheet.
2. Bake 6 to 8 minutes, until golden-brown. Leave to cool, then gently ease off the molds with the help of a knife. If the filo baskets stick, cook them a few minutes longer.
3. Cut the asparagus into 1-1/2-inch lengths and cook in boiling salted water 5 minutes; drain and set aside. In a pan, heat oil, add onion and fry until softened. Add garlic and mushrooms and cook 2 minutes, stirring occasionally. Remove from heat, stir in flour, then gradually add stock and tarragon. Bring to a boil, stirring, and cook 2 minutes. Add half and half, asparagus, chicken, nuts and seasoning.

Spoon filling into filo baskets. Serve on warmed individual plates, accompanied by broccoli.

Makes 4 servings.

Pheasant with Chestnuts

12 ounces chestnuts
1 tablespoon olive oil
1 (2-1/2- to 3-lb.) pheasant, cleaned
8 ounces pearl onions
2 tablespoons all-purpose flour
1-1/4 cups stock (made from pheasant giblets)
Grated peel and juice of 1/2 orange
1 tablespoon red currant jelly
2/3 cup red wine
Bouquet garni (see page 50)
Salt and pepper, to taste
CROÛTES:
2 slices bread, crusts removed
Vegetable oil
2 tablespoons chopped fresh parsley

1. Preheat oven to 350F (175C). Plunge the chestnuts into boiling water 2 minutes, then peel away skins. In a flameproof casserole dish, heat oil and brown pheasant all over until golden; remove. Add chestnuts and onions to casserole dish and cook 5 to 8 minutes, stirring, until beginning to turn golden-brown; remove from casserole dish.
2. Stir in flour, then gradually mix in stock and bring to a boil. Add orange peel and juice, red currant jelly, wine, bouquet garni and seasoning. Return pheasant, onions and chestnuts to casserole dish, cover and cook in the oven 1-1/2 hours, or until pheasant is tender.

3. Remove pheasant from casserole and arrange on a warmed shallow serving dish with onions and chestnuts; keep warm. Discard bouquet garni. Boil cooking liquid rapidly until reduced to a syrupy consistency.

To make croûtes, cut each bread slice into 4 triangles. Shallow-fry in hot oil until golden-brown. Dip one side of each croûte into the sauce, then into chopped parsley. Arrange around the pheasant. Spoon remaining sauce over pheasant and serve with braised red cabbage or brussels sprouts.

Makes 4 servings.

Stuffed Beef Rolls

4 smoked ham slices
8 thin beef slices, about 4 ounces each
2 tablespoons vegetable oil
2 garlic cloves, chopped
2 tablespoons all-purpose flour
1/2 cup beef stock
1 cup red wine
Bouquet garni (see page 50)
2 tomatoes, peeled, seeded and cut into strips
12 ripe olives, halved and pitted
STUFFING:
2/3 cup pitted prunes
1 cup fresh bread crumbs
1/4 cup grated Parmesan cheese
3 tablespoons chopped fresh parsley
2 tablespoons pine nuts

1. Preheat oven to 350F (175C). Cut ham slices in half lengthwise and put a piece on each slice of beef.

2. To make stuffing, chop prunes and put in a bowl with bread crumbs, Parmesan cheese, 2 tablespoons parsley and pine nuts; mix well. Divide equally between meat, roll up and tie with fine string.

3. In a flameproof casserole dish, heat oil and cook beef rolls, two at a time, turning to brown all over; re- move and set aside.

Add garlic and cook 1 minute; stir in flour. Pour in stock and wine, add bouquet garni and bring to a boil, stirring. Return rolls to casserole dish, cover and cook in the oven 1-1/4 hours. Add tomatoes and olives and cook 15 minutes. Turn into a serving dish, sprinkle with remaining parsley and serve with cooked tagliatelle.

Makes 4 servings.

Pork with Prunes

2 pork tenderloins, about 1-1/2 pounds total
1 cup pitted prunes
1/4 cup pistachios (1 ounce)
2 tablespoons olive oil
8 ounces pearl onions, peeled
1 tablespoon all-purpose flour
1-1/4 cups veal or chicken stock
1 cup red wine
Salt and pepper, to taste
2 teaspoons cornstarch, blended with a little water
1 tablespoon chopped fresh parsley

1. Make a horizontal cut along the length of each tenderloin, three-quarters of the way through the meat; open it out flat.

2. Lay 10 to 12 prunes down the center of one tenderloin, sprinkle with pistachios, and cover with second tenderloin. Tie tenderloins together securely with string. In an oval flameproof casserole dish, heat oil and brown meat and onions thoroughly all over. Stir in flour, then gradually mix in stock and wine. Bring to a boil, season, cover and simmer gently 35 to 40 minutes.

3. Add remaining prunes to the casserole; cook another 15 to 20 minutes. Lift meat from casserole with a slotted spoon. Carve into slices, remove string and arrange on a warm serving dish; keep hot. Remove onions and prunes with a slotted spoon; set aside. Strain cooking liquid, return to casserole dish and stir in blended cornstarch. Bring to a boil and cook, stirring, until thickened. Add prunes, onions and parsley, heat through, then spoon around the meat. Serve with braised red cabbage or celery.

Makes 6 servings.

Calves' Liver with Apple

1 cup dried apple rings, soaked 2 hours
4 tablespoons butter
1 teaspoon honey
1 pound calves' liver
2 tablespoons seasoned flour
1 tablespoon olive oil
1/2 cup veal or chicken stock
1/2 cup red wine
1 teaspoon chopped sage
1/4 cup pine nuts, toasted
TO GARNISH:
Sage leaves

1. Drain apple rings and pat dry with paper towels. In a medium-size skillet, melt half the butter and add honey. Fry apple rings in a single layer 4 to 5 minutes, turning once. Remove from pan and keep warm. Wipe out pan.
2. Coat liver slices completely with seasoned flour. Heat remaining butter and oil in pan. Add liver and fry 1 to 2 minutes on each side, depending on thickness. Add stock, wine and sage and cook 2 minutes. Remove liver with a slotted spoon; reserve cooking liquid.
3. Arrange liver and apple rings on a warm serving dish; keep warm. Boil reserved liquid 2 minutes to reduce slightly, then spoon over the liver. Sprinkle with pine nuts and garnish with sage to serve.

Makes 4 servings.

Moroccan Lamb Stew

3 tablespoons olive oil
1-1/2 pounds lean lamb, cut into 1-inch cubes
2 onions, sliced
2 garlic cloves, chopped
2 teaspoons chopped gingerroot
1 teaspoon ground cinnamon
1/2 teaspoon ground cloves
3 cardamom pods, split open
1 tablespoon plus 1 teaspoon all-purpose flour
1-3/4 cups beef stock
Grated peel and juice of 1/2 orange
Salt and pepper, to taste
1 thyme sprig
1 teaspoon each wine vinegar and brown sugar
1 cup dried apricots, soaked overnight
1/4 cup pistachios (1 ounce)

1. In a flameproof casserole dish, heat 2 tablespoons oil and fry meat briskly in batches until browned; remove from casserole dish and set aside. Add onions to casserole dish and fry until softened, then add garlic, gingerroot and spices and fry 1 minute.

2. Stir in flour, then stir in stock, orange peel and juice, seasoning, thyme, vinegar and sugar; bring to a boil. Return meat to the casserole, cover and simmer gently 30 minutes.

3. Drain apricots, add to casserole and simmer 30 minutes, until meat is tender. Serve sprinkled with pistachios and accompanied by couscous.

Makes 4 servings.

Spiced Pilaf

2/3 cup chopped dried apricots
4 tablespoons olive oil
1 onion, chopped
1 teaspoon ground allspice
1 garlic clove, chopped
1-1/2 cups long-grain rice
2-1/2 cups beef stock or water
Salt and pepper, to taste
1 cup fresh bread crumbs
1 pound lean ground lamb
1 tablespoon tomato paste
1 teaspoon ground cumin
1 egg, beaten
1/2 cup pine nuts
2 tablespoons chopped parsley

1. Cover apricots with boiling water and let soak 1 hour; drain well.

In a large saucepan, heat 2 tablespoons oil, add onion and fry until softened. Add allspice, garlic and rice and fry, stirring, 1 to 2 minutes. Add stock, bring to a boil, add salt and pepper, reduce heat, cover and cook gently 15 minutes, until liquid has been absorbed.

2. Meanwhile, soak bread crumbs in 1/2 cup water 5 minutes; squeeze dry and place in a bowl. Add lamb, tomato paste, cumin, egg and seasoning and mix together thoroughly. With dampened hands, roll into balls, each the size of a large marble.

3. In a medium-size skillet, heat remaining oil, add pine nuts and fry, turning constantly, until golden-brown; remove from pan. Add meatballs to pan and fry quickly 5 to 8 minutes, until golden all over.

Meanwhile, add apricots to cooked rice mixture, cover and heat through. Fluff rice and arrange on warm plates. Spoon meatballs on top and sprinkle with pine nuts and parsley to serve.

Makes 4 servings.

Brazil Nut & Cranberry Loaf

2 celery stalks
1 onion, chopped
3 tablespoons vegetable oil
1 garlic clove, crushed
2 tablespoons all-purpose flour
1 (7-oz.) can chopped tomatoes
3/4 cup Brazil nuts, chopped
2 cups whole-wheat bread crumbs
4 ounces cranberries
1 tablespoon plus 1 teaspoon soy sauce
2 tablespoons chopped parsley
1 egg, beaten
4 green onions
1 teaspoon red currant jelly
3/4 cup vegetable or chicken stock
1/4 cup port

1. Preheat oven to 350F (175C). Grease and line a 9" x 5" loaf pan. Chop celery and onion. In a medium saucepan, heat 2 tablespoons oil, add onion and fry until softened. Add celery and garlic and fry 3 minutes, stirring occasionally. Mix in 1 tablespoon flour, then add tomatoes and cook until thickened, stirring.

2. Add the nuts, bread crumbs, half the cranberries, 1 tablespoon soy sauce, the parsley and egg. Season with salt and pepper to taste, and mix well. Turn into prepared pan, cover with foil and bake 1 hour.

3. To make the sauce, chop the green onions diagonally, keeping green and white parts separate. In a small pan, heat remaining oil and fry white part of green onions 1 minute. Mix in remaining 1 tablespoon flour and red currant jelly, then gradually stir in the stock and port. Bring to a boil, stirring, then add remaining soy sauce, cranberries, green part of green onions and pepper to taste; cook 5 minutes.

Turn out nut loaf, cut into slices with a sharp knife and serve with the cranberry sauce. Accompany with snow peas.

Makes 4 servings.

Hazelnut Croquettes

6 large dried cloud ear mushrooms
6 tablespoons sunflower oil
1 onion, chopped
3 garlic cloves, chopped
1 celery stalk, chopped
2 teaspoons ground coriander
1/4 cup all-purpose flour
1 tablespoon soy sauce
Scant cup hazelnuts, ground
2 cups fresh bread crumbs
2 tablespoons chopped parsley

MUSHROOM SAUCE:
1 tablespoon butter
2 tablespoons sherry
1/4 cup whipping cream
1 teaspoon chopped fresh thyme
2 teaspoons cornstarch

1. Soak mushrooms in boiling water to cover 30 minutes; drain, reserving 2/3 cup liquid. Finely chop half the mushrooms; slice remaining mushrooms. Set all mushrooms aside.

2. In a medium-size saucepan, heat 2 tablespoons oil, add onion, 2 garlic cloves and celery; fry gently until softened. Add coriander and fry 1 minute, then stir in 2 tablespoons flour. Off the heat, stir in reserved mushroom liquid and soy sauce. Bring to a boil and cook 2 minutes, until thickened. Add chopped mushrooms, ground hazelnuts, bread crumbs, parsley and seasoning; mix thoroughly.

3. Season remaining flour. Divide nut mixture into 12 portions and, us-ing dampened hands, shape into croquettes. Roll in seasoned flour to coat. Heat remaining oil in a medium-size skillet; add croquettes. Fry about 2 minutes on each side, until golden-brown and crisp. Keep warm while making sauce.

In a small saucepan, melt the butter and quickly fry remaining sliced mushrooms and garlic. Add sherry, 2 tablespoons water, cream and thyme; cover and simmer 5 minutes. Blend cornstarch with 1/2 cup water; stir into sauce. Bring to a boil, stirring, and cook 1 minute. Serve the croquettes with the sauce, and accompany with French beans.

Makes 4 servings.

Broccoli & Blue Cheese Salad

12 ounces broccoli
1 red apple, quartered and cored
1/2 cup slivered almonds, toasted
DRESSING:
2 ounces blue cheese, softened
2/3 cup plain yogurt
1 tablespoon chopped parsley
1 tablespoon snipped chives
Salt and pepper, to taste

1. Divide broccoli into flowerets. Bring a large saucepan of water to a boil, add broccoli and cook 4 minutes. Drain, rinse in cold water and drain again thoroughly.

2. To make dressing, put blue cheese on a plate and mash it with a fork. Scrape into a bowl and gradually beat in yogurt to make a smooth paste. Add parsley, chives and seasoning. Mix thoroughly.

3. Turn dressing into a bowl and thinly slice the apple into it. Mix together until well coated, then mix into broccoli with three-quarters of the nuts. Turn into individual dishes and sprinkle with remaining nuts. Serve as a delicious accompaniment to cold meats.

Makes 4 servings.

Bacon & Watercress Salad

2 red-skinned apples, quartered and cored
1 bunch of watercress
2 heads of Belgian endive
LEMON DRESSING:
3 tablespoons olive oil
1 tablespoon lemon juice
1/2 teaspoon honey
Salt and pepper, to taste
TO GARNISH:
4 bacon slices
1/2 cup macadamia nuts, toasted

1. First, make dressing: put all ingredients in a jar with a tight-fitting lid and shake thoroughly until blended; pour into a large bowl.

Slice apples thinly into dressing; toss thoroughly to coat and prevent discoloration.

2. Break watercress into sprigs; cut Belgian endive into diagonal slices; add both to bowl and toss again. Turn into a salad bowl.

3. To prepare garnish, cut bacon into strips and cook in a nonstick skillet until crisp. Sprinkle bacon and nuts over salad.

Serve immediately, as a light starter or delicious salad accompaniment.

Makes 4 servings.

Variation: Replace Belgian endive with 1 head of radicchio, torn into bite-size pieces.

Cauliflower & Avocado Salad

8 ounces shelled broad beans or fresh lima beans
12 ounces cauliflowerets
1 avocado
DRESSING:
2 ounces blue cheese
5 tablespoons half and half
1/4 cup chopped walnuts
Salt and pepper, to taste
Little milk (optional)
TO GARNISH:
1/4 cup chopped walnuts
Parsley sprigs

1. Bring a large saucepan of salted water to a boil, add broad beans and cook 6 minutes. Add cauliflower, bring back to a boil, and cook 2 minutes. Drain thoroughly and let cool.
2. To make dressing, put cheese, half and half, nuts and seasoning in a blender or food processor fitted with the metal blade and process until smooth. Turn into a bowl and thin with a little milk if necessary.

Halve, pit and peel avocado, then slice, adding to the dressing; mix gently to coat.
3. Add to beans and cauliflower, mix again gently, then turn into individual serving dishes. Garnish with walnuts and parsley to serve, as an accompaniment.

Makes 4 servings.

Variation: Sprinkle with crisply fried chopped bacon as well as, or instead of, chopped walnuts.

Salade Tiède

1/4 head chicory
1/4 head oak leaf lettuce
Few radicchio leaves
Handful of arugula leaves or corn salad (lamb's lettuce)
1 head of Belgian endive
2 tablespoons walnut oil
8 ounces duck livers, cut into slices
2 tablespoons sherry vinegar or raspberry vinegar
Salt and pepper, to taste
TO GARNISH:
1/2 cup pecans
Edible flowers (optional)

1. Tear chicory, lettuce and radicchio into bite-size pieces and put into 4 individual salad bowls with the arugula leaves. Slice Belgian endive into diagonal slices and add to bowls.

2. In a medium-size skillet, heat oil and fry livers 2 to 3 minutes, turning occasionally to cook evenly. Add to the salads with the oil and juices from the pan.

3. Add vinegar to saucepan and stir to deglaze. Pour a little over each salad, season with salt and pepper and toss well. Sprinkle nuts and flowers, if desired, over each bowl.

Serve as a delicious starter, or light lunch with crusty bread.

Makes 4 servings.

Variation: Use chicken livers instead of duck livers.

Apple Coleslaw

6 tablespoons plain yogurt
1 tablespoon lemon juice
1 teaspoon Dijon-style mustard
Salt and pepper, to taste
2 red-skinned apples, quartered, cored and chopped
8 ounces white cabbage
1/2 cup raisins
3/4 cup coarsely chopped hazelnuts, toasted
2 celery stalks, chopped
2 tablespoons chopped parsley

1. In a medium-size bowl, mix together yogurt, lemon juice, mustard and seasoning; add apples and mix until thoroughly coated with the dressing.

2. Remove any core from cabbage and shred finely with a mandolin or in a food processor.

3. Add raisins, hazelnuts, celery, parsley and shredded cabbage to the apples. Toss the salad thoroughly un- til all the ingredients are coated with dressing. Turn into a salad bowl to serve.

Makes 6 servings.

Variations: Use snipped chives instead of chopped parsley. Chopped dates make a good substitute for raisins. Walnuts can be used instead of hazelnuts.

Oriental Chicken Salad

9 ounces cooked skinned chicken breast halves
1 red bell pepper, thinly sliced
6 ounces snow peas, trimmed
1 (7-oz.) can water chestnuts, drained
1/2 cup slivered almonds, toasted
4 ounces mushrooms, sliced
DRESSING:
2 tablespoons tahini
2 tablespoons rice vinegar or wine vinegar
2 tablespoons medium-dry sherry
1 teaspoon sesame oil
1 tablespoon soy sauce
1 garlic clove, crushed

1. First, make dressing: put tahini in a small bowl and gradually mix in rice vinegar and sherry. Add oil, soy sauce and garlic and mix together thoroughly.

2. Cut chicken into 1/4-inch-wide strips and put in a medium-size bowl with bell pepper.

3. Cut snow peas in half diagonally if large. Blanch in boiling water 3 minutes; drain and rinse under cold running water to preserve color.

Slice water chestnuts thinly and add to chicken with snow peas, almonds and mushrooms. Pour over dressing and toss well.

Spoon the salad into a shallow serving dish and serve, as a main course salad, with crusty bread.

Makes 4 servings.

Date & Apple Crunch

4 Pippin apples, quartered and cored
3/4 cup chopped dates
1 red bell pepper, diced
4 celery stalks, chopped
3/4 cup coarsely chopped hazelnuts, toasted
DRESSING:
2 tablespoons olive oil
2 teaspoons lemon juice
2 teaspoons Dijon-style mustard
Salt and pepper, to taste
TO GARNISH:
2 heads of Belgian endive, separated into leaves

1. First, make dressing: put all ingredients in a jar with a tight-fitting lid and shake thoroughly until emulsified; pour into a medium-size bowl.
2. Chop apples and add to dressing; mix well to prevent discoloration.
3. Add remaining ingredients to bowl and toss well. Pile salad into the center of a flat serving plate. Tuck Belgian endive under the edge of the salad all the way around, to make a sunflower design.

Makes 6 to 8 servings.

Note: This salad is ideal to serve in the winter, especially at Christmas time. If you prefer, serve the salad on individual plates—you will need an extra head or two of Belgian endive for the "sunflower" pattern.

Variation: Toss the salad ingredients with a lemon-flavored mayonnaise: mix together 5 tablespoons mayonnaise, 4 tablespoons plain yogurt and 1 tablespoon lemon juice with seasoning to taste, and use instead of the above dressing.

Wild Rice Salad

3/4 cup chopped dried apricots
2 tablespoons wild rice
1/2 cup brown rice
4 ounces button mushrooms, sliced
2 celery stalks, sliced
1 cup pistachios (4 ounces)
DRESSING:
1 tablespoon hazelnut oil
3 tablespoons sunflower oil
1 tablespoon raspberry wine vinegar
1/2 teaspoon ground coriander
Salt and pepper, to taste
1/2 teaspoon honey

1. Cover apricots with boiling water, soak 1 hour, then drain well; set aside.

Bring a large saucepan of salted water to a boil, add wild rice and cook 10 minutes; add brown rice and cook 30 to 40 minutes, until tender. Rinse and drain thoroughly; set aside.

2. Put all dressing ingredients into a jar with a tight-fitting lid and shake vigorously to mix. Pour into a medium-size bowl.

3. Add mushrooms to bowl and toss until thoroughly coated with dressing. Add celery, pistachios, apricots and rice; mix well. Turn into a salad bowl and serve as an accompaniment. This delicious salad goes particularly well with cold duck or game.

Makes 4 servings.

Mango & Passion Fruit Molds

4 ounces dried mango
2-1/2 cups apple juice
1 teaspoon lemon juice
3 passion fruit, halved
3 tablespoons Cointreau
2 tablespoons cold water
1 tablespoon plus 2 teaspoons plain gelatin powder
3/4 cup whipping cream
TO DECORATE:
Mint sprigs

1. Put mango and apple juice in a bowl and soak overnight.

Transfer mango and juice to a saucepan, bring to a boil, reduce heat, cover and simmer 10 minutes, until tender. Cool slightly, then transfer to a blender or food processor fitted with the metal blade, add lemon juice and process to a puree; add a little water to make up to 3 cups if necessary. Scoop out seeds and flesh from 2 passion fruit into a sieve; press through as much juice as possible and add to mango puree with the Cointreau.

2. Put 2 tablespoons cold water in a small saucepan, add gelatin and let stand 5 minutes, until softened. Heat very gently until dissolved; stir into mango mixture. Pour into 6 (1/2-cup) molds and refrigerate until set.

3. Scoop seeds and pulp from remaining passion fruit into a cup.

To turn out molds, quickly dip into hot water to loosen and invert onto individual serving plates. Surround each mold with cream. Dot passion fruit into cream, and decorate molds with mint sprigs.

Makes 6 servings.

Summer Fruits & Peach Coulis

1/2 cup dried peaches
1-1/4 cups apple juice
3 tablespoons apricot brandy
2 figs
2 kiwifruit
1 nectarine
4 ounces strawberries
4 ounces raspberries
4 ounces red currants
4 ounces shredded coconut
TO DECORATE:
Mint sprigs and/or salad burnet

1. Put peaches and apple juice in a bowl and soak overnight.

Transfer peaches and juice to a saucepan, bring to a boil and simmer 15 minutes; cool. Process to a puree in a blender or food processor fitted with the metal blade; turn into a medium-size bowl and stir in apricot brandy.

2. Cut the figs into quarters. Peel and slice kiwifruit. Slice nectarine and halve strawberries. Leave the raspberries whole and red currants on stems.

3. Put a pool of peach sauce on 4 individual serving plates and arrange the fruits attractively on top. Sprinkle with shredded coconut and decorate with mint and/or salad burnet.

Makes 4 servings.

Apricots with Orange

8 ounces apricots
2/3 cup orange juice
1-1/4 cups boiling water
2 tablespoons Cointreau
3 oranges
1/4 cup pistachios (1 ounce)

1. Put apricots, orange juice and water in a saucepan and soak 2 hours. Bring to a boil, cover and simmer gently 10 minutes. Transfer to a bowl, add Cointreau and cool.

2. Cut 4 thin strips of orange peel with a vegetable peeler and cut into needle-fine shreds. Blanch in boiling water 1 minute; drain and dry on paper towels. Set aside.

3. Peel oranges with a serrated knife and cut into sections, removing all membrane. Add to apricots and mix gently. Transfer to individual serving dishes and sprinkle with pistachios and shredded orange peel to serve.

Makes 4 servings.

Variation: Use 8 ounces strawberries in place of oranges.

Syrian Fruit Salad

1-3/4 cups dried apricots
2/3 cup prunes
1/3 cup raisins
1/4 cup pine nuts, toasted
1/4 cup pistachios (1 ounce), roughly chopped
1/4 cup slivered almonds, toasted
1 tablespoon rose water
1 pomegranate

1. Put apricots, prunes and raisins in a medium-size bowl, cover with 3 cups water and soak overnight.

Pour fruit and soaking liquid into a saucepan, bring to a boil, reduce heat, cover and simmer 15 minutes; cool.

2. Transfer to a serving bowl and sprinkle with pine nuts, pistachios, almonds and rose water.

3. Halve pomegranate and scoop out seeds using a teaspoon; sprinkle over fruit salad. Cover and refrigerate until required. Serve the fruit salad with plain yogurt.

Makes 6 servings.

Variation: Use dried peaches and figs instead of the apricots and prunes if you prefer.

Crème aux Pruneaux

**10 ounces fromage frais or 1/4 cup plain yogurt and 1
(8-oz.) package cream cheese, softened
1 tablespoon honey
2/3 cup whipping cream
PRUNE SAUCE:
2/3 cup pitted prunes
1-7/8 cups apple juice
TO DECORATE:
2 tablespoons half and half
Lemon balm sprigs**

  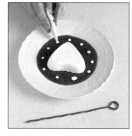

1. Mix fromage frais or yogurt and cream cheese and honey together until smooth. Whip cream until it forms soft peaks; fold into cheese mixture.
2. Line 6 heart-shaped molds with cheesecloth; spoon in cheese mixture and smooth the tops. Put on a plate and refrigerate overnight. Soak prunes in apple juice overnight too.
3. To make sauce, put prunes and apple juice into a medium-size saucepan, bring to a boil, reduce heat, cover and simmer 15 minutes. Cool

slightly, then transfer to a blender or food processor fitted with the metal blade and process to a puree; pour into a pitcher and allow to cool.

Unmold hearts out on individual plates; pour prune sauce around. Put half and half into a plastic bag and drop small dots of half and half into the sauce around the heart. Swirl with a skewer into an attractive design. Decorate with lemon balm to serve.

Makes 6 servings.

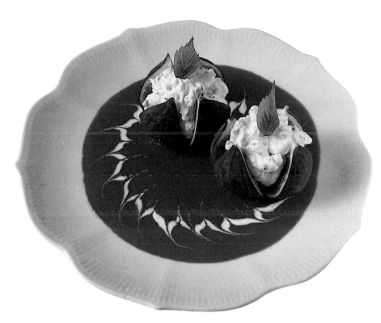

Figs with Praline

2/3 cup whipping cream
8 figs
PRALINE:
1/4 cup whole unblanched almonds
2 tablespoons superfine sugar
MELBA SAUCE:
8 ounces raspberries
2 tablespoons powdered sugar, sifted
TO DECORATE:
Mint leaves

1. First make praline: put almonds and sugar in a small saucepan and heat until sugar has melted. Cook, shaking saucepan occasionally, until a good caramel color. Turn onto an oiled baking sheet and cool until hard. Crush with a rolling pin and set aside.

2. Whip all but 2 tablespoons cream until it holds its shape; fold in praline.

Cut a deep cross in the top of each fig and open out slightly. Put a generous spoonful of praline cream in the center of each fig; set aside.

3. To make Melba sauce, put raspberries and powdered sugar in a blender or food processor fitted with the metal blade and process to a puree; rub through a sieve to remove seeds.

Pour a pool of Melba sauce onto 4 individual plates. Put dots of remaining cream on sauce and swirl into a pattern with a skewer. Arrange 2 figs on each plate and decorate with mint to serve.

Makes 4 servings.

Petits Vacherins aux Abricots

MERINGUE:
2 egg whites
3/4 cup light brown sugar
1/2 cup pecans, ground
FILLING:
1/2 cup dried apricots, soaked overnight
1 cup whipping cream
2 tablespoons apricot brandy
TO FINISH:
8 pecans

1. Preheat oven to 275F (135C). Line 2 baking sheets with parchment paper and draw 8 (3-inch) circles and 8 (2-inch) circles on the paper.

Whisk egg whites until stiff; gradually whisk in sugar. Carefully fold in ground nuts with a large metal spoon.

2. Put meringue in a pastry bag fitted with a 1/2-inch plain tip and pipe onto the circles to cover completely. Bake 1-1/2 to 2 hours. Transfer meringue rounds to a wire rack to cool.

To prepare filling, put apricots and soaking liquid in a small saucepan, bring to a boil, cover and cook 20 minutes. Drain, chop and set aside.

3. Whip cream and apricot brandy together until it forms stiff peaks; put a quarter of the cream in a pastry bag fitted with a large fluted tip. Fold apricots into remaining cream and spread over the larger meringue circles. Cover with the smaller circles. Pipe a whirl of cream on top of each vacherin and decorate with a pecan.

Makes 8 servings.

Hazelnut Galettes with Mango

6 tablespoons butter
1/3 cup light brown sugar
1 cup all-purpose flour, sifted
2/3 cup hazelnuts, toasted and ground
1-1/4 cups whipping cream
MANGO SAUCE:
4 ounces dried mango, soaked overnight
2 passion fruit, halved
TO DECORATE:
Pineapple mint sprigs

1. Preheat oven to 350F (175C). In a bowl, cream butter and sugar together until light and fluffy; stir in flour and hazelnuts and mix to a firm dough, using your hand.

On a floured surface, knead lightly until smooth, then roll out thinly and cut out 8 (3-inch) circles and 8 (2-inch) circles. Place on a baking sheet and bake 12 to 15 minutes, until golden. Transfer to a wire rack to cool.

2. To make sauce, put mango and soaking liquid in a saucepan, cover and cook 15 minutes. Drain, reserving liquid; chop mango and set half aside. Put half the mango pieces and 1/3 to 1/2 cup reserved liquid in a blender or food processor fitted with the metal blade and process to a thin puree. Sieve passion fruit and add juice to mango sauce.

3. Whip cream until it forms stiff peaks; put one-fourth in a pastry bag fitted with a large fluted tip. Mix the reserved chopped mango with remaining cream; spread over the large pastry rounds. Cover with smaller rounds and pipe a rosette of cream on top. Spoon 2 tablespoons mango sauce onto 8 serving plates and place a galette on each. Decorate with mint.

Makes 8 servings.

Almond & Apricot Cornets

COOKIE MIXTURE:
1/4 cup all-purpose flour
1/4 cup sugar
1 egg white
2 tablespoons butter, melted
2 tablespoons slivered almonds
FILLING:
1-1/3 cups dried apricots, soaked overnight
2/3 cup whipping cream
1/4 cup crushed Amaretti cookies
TO DECORATE:
Frosted mint leaves (see page 97)

1. Preheat oven to 400F (205C). Grease and flour 3 baking sheets.

Put flour and sugar in a bowl; make a well in the center, add egg white and butter and beat until smooth. Put dessertspoons of the mixture onto prepared baking sheets, spread out thinly into 5-inch rounds, and sprinkle with almonds. Bake 6 to 7 minutes, until pale golden; only bake 3 at a time or they will begin to set before you roll them up.

2. Remove from baking sheet with a thin spatula and curl around cornet molds, holding in position until set; remove from molds.

3. To prepare filling: put apricots and their soaking liquid in a saucepan and cook 20 minutes; drain, reserving liquid. Put two-thirds of the apricots and 3/4 cup reserved liquid in a blender or food processor fitted with the metal blade and process to a puree. Chop remaining apricots. Whip cream and fold in chopped apricots and Amaretti crumbs. Spoon into prepared cornets.

Decorate with frosted leaves and serve with apricot sauce.

Makes 6 servings.

Note: The cookie mixture makes 9 cornets, which allows for breakages.

Red Currant & Nut Tartlets

1 cup all-purpose flour
1/4 cup butter, chilled
1 tablespoon plus 2 teaspoons sugar
1/2 cup hazelnuts, ground
1 to 2 tablespoons milk
FILLING:
1 (8-oz.) package cream cheese, softened
1 tablespoon sugar
Grated peel and juice of 1/2 lemon
SAUCE:
12 ounces red currants
1/4 cup sugar
TO DECORATE:
Frosted leaves (see page 97)

1. Sift flour into a bowl and cut in butter until mixture resembles bread crumbs. Stir in sugar and hazelnuts; add enough milk to mix to a firm dough. Knead lightly on a floured surface; refrigerate 15 minutes.
2. Preheat oven to 400F (205C). On a lightly floured surface, roll out pastry thinly and use it to line 12 patty pans; prick bottoms with a fork, press a square of foil into each tartlet case and refrigerate 15 minutes. Bake 10 minutes; remove foil and cook 5 minutes.
3. To make filling, mix cheese, sugar, lemon peel and juice in a bowl; spoon into tartlets.

To make sauce, put the red currants in a saucepan with the sugar and 2 tablespoons water. Cover and simmer 5 minutes. Set aside one-fourth of the red currants for decoration. Rub the remainder through a sieve and cool.

Arrange a few red currants on top of each tartlet and decorate with frosted leaves. Spoon the red currant sauce onto 6 individual plates and arrange 2 tartlets on each plate to serve.

Makes 6 servings.

Fruit Parcels & Brandy Cream

1 eating apple
1/4 cup mincemeat
1 teaspoon grated orange peel
1 sheet filo pastry
1 tablespoon butter, melted
Vegetable oil for deep-frying
BRANDY CREAM:
2/3 cup half and half
3 tablespoons brandy
TO DECORATE:
Powdered sugar for sprinkling
Candied orange peel

1. Quarter, core and chop apple; put in a small bowl with the mincemeat and orange peel and mix together thoroughly.

2. Cut filo pastry into 24 (3-inch) squares; pile on top of each other and cover with a clean towel to prevent pastry from drying out. Take one pastry square, brush with butter and lay another square on top; brush with butter. Set aside. Repeat with remaining pastry.

3. Put a small mound of mincemeat mixture in the center of each pastry square, then bring up edges of pastry and pinch together into a "money bag" shape; the butter will help the pastry to stick.

In a deep pan, heat oil until a cube of bread turns brown in 60 seconds. Put 3 parcels in a frying basket and deep-fry 1 minute, until crisp and golden-brown, turning once; drain thoroughly on paper towels. Repeat with remaining parcels.

To make brandy cream, mix half and half and brandy together; put 2 tablespoons on each serving plate. Place 3 fruit parcels on each plate and sprinkle with powdered sugar. Decorate with candied orange peel.

Makes 4 servings.

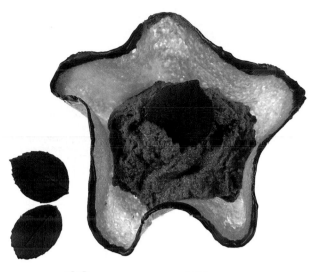

Chestnut Tulips

COOKIE MIXTURE:
1/4 cup all-purpose flour, sifted
1/4 cup sugar
1 egg white
2 tablespoons butter, melted
2 ounces semisweet chocolate, chopped
CHESTNUT FILLING:
4 ounces semisweet chocolate, in pieces
1/3 cup half and half
8 ounces peeled, cooked chestnuts, sieved (see page 38)
2 tablespoons Grand Marnier
2/3 cup whipping cream
TO DECORATE:
Chocolate rose leaves (see page 98)

1. Make and cook cookie mixture, as for Almond Cornets (see page 90), omitting almonds. Remove from baking sheets with a thin spatula and invert each one over the bottom of an upturned glass. Mold to give wavy edges, let harden, then remove carefully.

2. Put chocolate in a dish over a saucepan of hot water until melted. Dip the wavy edge of each biscuit into the chocolate, rotating until coated; set aside to dry.

3. To make filling, heat chocolate and half and half in a pan, until melted.

Put in a blender or food processor fitted with the metal blade with chestnuts and Grand Marnier and process until smooth; turn into a bowl. Whip whipping cream and carefully fold into chestnut mixture.

Spoon filling into cookies just before serving and decorate with chocolate rose leaves.

Makes 6 servings.

Note: The cookie mixture makes 9 cookies; this allows for 3 breakages, as they are delicate.

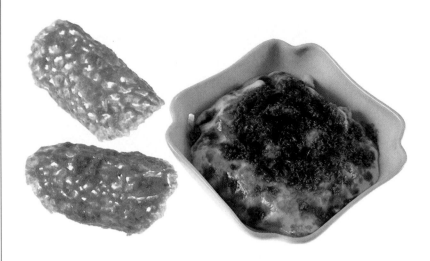

Mango Brûlée with Nut Curls

1/2 cup dried mango, soaked overnight
3/4 cup whipping cream
3/4 cup plain yogurt
1/3 cup light brown sugar
NUT CURLS:
3 tablespoons butter
2 tablespoons plus 2 teaspoons sugar
1/4 cup all-purpose flour, sifted
1/4 cup slivered almonds

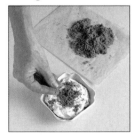

1. Put mango and soaking liquid in a saucepan, bring to a boil, and cook 5 minutes; drain thoroughly. Whip cream until soft peaks form, then fold in yogurt. Add mango and stir to combine.

2. Turn into 4 ramekins or other individual ovenproof dishes and sprinkle thickly with brown sugar. Preheat oven to 375F (190C).

3. To make nut curls, in a small bowl cream butter and sugar together until light and fluffy; stir in flour and almonds and mix well. Place 12 to 14 teaspoons of the mixture well apart on baking sheets and flatten with a spatula. Bake 6 to 8 minutes, until pale golden. Cool 1 minute, then remove with a spatula and place on a rolling pin to curl, until set.

Put the mango creams under a preheated hot broiler 1 to 2 minutes, until caramelized. Serve with the nut curls.

Makes 4 servings.

Hazelnut Ice & Chocolate Sauce

1 cup fresh whole-wheat bread crumbs
1/4 cup light brown sugar
2/3 cup hazelnuts, ground
3 egg whites
1/2 cup sugar
1-1/4 cups whipping cream
CHOCOLATE SAUCE:
4 ounces semisweet chocolate, chopped
1-1/4 cups half and half

1. Mix bread crumbs, brown sugar and ground hazelnuts together on a baking sheet; broil under medium heat until golden-brown, stirring occasionally to ensure the mixture browns evenly. Cool.

2. Whisk egg whites until stiff; gradually whisk in sugar. Whip whipping cream. Carefully fold hazelnut mixture and cream into egg white mixture; turn into a freezerproof container, cover, seal and freeze 4 hours, until firm.

To make sauce, put chocolate and all but 2 tablespoons half and half in a saucepan and heat very gently until melted. Stir to mix; leave to cool.

3. One hour before serving, scoop out balls of ice cream, using a melon baller; place on a baking sheet and return to freezer until required. Spoon chocolate sauce onto 6 individual plates. Fill a paper pastry bag with remaining half and half, snip off the end and drizzle a spiral on each pool of sauce. Use a skewer to create feathered designs. Arrange hazelnut ice cream balls on the sauce and serve immediately.

Makes 6 servings.

Glacé Fruit Bombes

2 ounces crystallized papaya
2 ounces crystallized pineapple
1 ounce angelica
2 ounces glacé pears
1/3 cup glacé cherries
2 ounces glacé apricots
3 tablespoons brandy
3 egg yolks
1/3 cup sugar
1-1/4 cups half and half
1-1/4 cups whipping cream
TO DECORATE:
Slivers of glacé pear or apricot

1. Chop papaya, pineapple and angelica; core and chop pears; quarter cherries; pit and chop apricots. Put papaya, pineapple and angelica in a bowl, add boiling water to cover and leave 10 minutes to soften and remove excess sugar. Drain thoroughly, then put in a bowl with remaining glacé fruits. Add brandy and soak 2 hours.

2. Beat egg yolks and sugar together until creamy. Bring half and half to a boil and pour onto egg mixture, mixing vigorously. Pour into a double boiler over a saucepan of simmering water and heat gently until thickened. Strain and cool.

3. Whip whipping cream until fairly thick and fold into the cooled custard. Pour into a rigid freezerproof container, cover, seal and freeze 2 hours, until half-frozen. Stir well, then fold in soaked fruit with any brandy that has not been absorbed. Press into a 2-cup bombe mold, cover with a lid or foil and freeze 2 to 3 hours until firm. Cut into wedges and decorate with glacé fruit.

Makes 6 servings.

Duet of Sorbets

PEAR SORBET:
8 ounces dried pears, soaked overnight
1/4 cup sugar
2 tablespoons pear liqueur
1 egg white
MANGO SORBET:
6 ounces dried mango, soaked overnight
1/4 cup sugar
2 passion fruit, halved and sieved
1 egg white
TO DECORATE:
Frosted mint leaves (see below)

1. To make pear sorbet, put pears in a saucepan with 1-3/4 cups of the soaking liquid, cover and simmer gently 15 minutes; stir in sugar. Pour into a blender or food processor fitted with the metal blade and process until smooth. Pour into a rigid freezerproof container and leave to cool. Add liqueur, cover, seal and freeze about 3 hours, until half-frozen.

2. Whisk egg white until stiff. Add half-frozen sorbet and whisk together until smooth. Return to freezerproof container, cover, seal and freeze 2 hours, until firm.

Make mango sorbet as above, substituting mango for pears, and passion fruit for liqueur.

3. One hour before serving, scoop out balls of each sorbet, using a melon baller; put on a baking sheet and return to the freezer until required. (Press down any remaining sorbet in container and keep for another occasion.) Arrange a mixture of sorbet balls on chilled individual plates and decorate with mint to serve.

Makes 8 to 10 servings.

Frosted mint leaves: Brush leaves with egg white, dip into sugar to coat evenly. Shake off excess sugar and allow to dry.

Chocolate & Chestnut Dessert

8 ounces semisweet chocolate, in pieces
1/4 cup cold water
1/2 cup butter, softened
3/4 cup light brown sugar
1 (15-oz.) can unsweetened chestnut purée
3 tablespoons brandy
TO DECORATE:
1/2 cup whipping cream
8 chocolate rose leaves (see below)

1. Grease an 8" x 4" loaf pan. Put chocolate and 1/4 cup cold water in a small saucepan over low heat until melted; cool. Put butter, sugar and chestnut puree in a blender or food processor fitted with the metal blade and process until smooth; add chocolate and brandy and process again. Turn into prepared pan, smooth the surface with a spatula, cover and refrigerate overnight.
2. To make chocolate rose leaves, choose leaves with clearly marked veins. Coat the underside of each leaf with melted chocolate, using a fine paint brush. Allow to set, chocolate side up, then paint on a second coat and allow to set. Carefully lift the tip of the leaf and peel away from the chocolate.
3. Whip cream until stiff; put into a pastry bag fitted with a fluted tip. Turn out dessert, cut into slices and arrange on individual serving dishes. Decorate with piped cream rosettes and chocolate rose leaves to serve.

Makes 8 servings.

Chestnut & Orange Roll

1 large orange
8 ounces peeled, cooked chestnuts, sieved (see page 38)
or 1 (15-oz.) can unsweetened chestnut puree
3 eggs, separated
3/4 cup light brown sugar
2 tablespoons powdered sugar
1-2/3 cup whipping cream
1/4 cup Cointreau

1. Preheat oven to 350F (175C). Grease and line a 13" x 9" baking pan, extending paper 1/2 inch above sides.

Cut a few strips of peel from the orange, cut into shreds and blanch 1 minute; drain and set aside. Squeeze juice from orange. In a blender or food processor fitted with the metal blade, process 2 tablespoons orange juice with sieved chestnuts, chestnut puree, egg yolks and brown sugar. Turn into a large bowl.

2. Whisk egg whites until fairly stiff; fold 2 tablespoons into chestnut mixture to lighten it, then carefully fold in remainder. Turn into prepared pan and spread evenly. Bake 20 to 25 minutes, until firm. Cool slightly, then cover with a clean damp towel and cool.

3. Sift powdered sugar onto a sheet of waxed paper; turn cake onto it, then peel off lining paper. Whip 1 cup whipping cream with 2 tablespoons Cointreau, spread over cake and roll up like a jellyroll.

To make sauce, mix remaining Cointreau and orange juice with grated peel and remaining whipping cream. Pour onto individual plates, place a slice of cake on top and decorate with orange peel shreds.

Makes 8 servings.

Apricot & Almond Flan

ALMOND PASTRY:
1-1/2 cups all-purpose flour
6 tablespoons butter or margarine, chilled
1/2 cup ground almonds
2 tablespoons sugar
1 egg yolk
APRICOT FILLING & SAUCE:
1-1/3 cups dried apricots, soaked overnight
1-1/4 cups apple juice
1 egg
1/4 cup butter, softened
3 tablespoons superfine sugar
1-1/4 cups ground almonds
2 drops almond extract
2 tablespoons apricot brandy
Powdered sugar

1. Sift flour into a bowl and cut in butter until mixture resembles bread crumbs; stir in ground almonds and sugar. Add egg yolk and 2 to 3 tablespoons water, mixing to a firm dough. Knead lightly on a floured surface until smooth; cover and refrigerate 20 minutes. Roll out three-quarters of the dough and use to line an 8-inch flan pan placed on a baking sheet. Refrigerate 30 minutes.

2. Preheat oven to 400F (205C). To make filling, drain apricots and cook in apple juice 10 minutes; drain, reserving 6 tablespoons liquid, and chop. In a bowl, beat egg, butter, sugar, ground almonds and almond extract together until smooth. Put half the apricots in prepared flan pan; spoon almond mixture over top.

3. Roll out remaining pastry thinly, cut into strips and use to make a lattice pattern over filling, moistening edges. Bake 15 minutes; reduce temperature to 375F (190C) and bake 15 to 20 minutes, until firm to the touch and golden. Cool.

To make sauce, blend remaining apricots, reserved liquid and brandy in a blender until smooth. Remove flan from pan, sprinkle with powdered sugar and serve with apricot sauce.

Makes 8 servings.

Praline & Apricot Cake

3 eggs, separated
1/2 cup sugar
Grated peel and juice of 1 lemon
1/3 cup semolina
1/4 cup ground almonds
PRALINE:
1/3 cup whole unblanched almonds
1/4 cup sugar
FILLING:
2/3 cup dried apricots, soaked overnight
1-1/4 cups whipping cream
TO DECORATE:
Candied apricot slices

1. Preheat oven to 350F (175C). Grease, line and flour an 8-inch cake pan.

Beat egg yolks with sugar, lemon peel and juice until thick; stir in semolina and ground almonds. Whisk egg whites until stiff; carefully fold into mixture. Turn into prepared pan and bake 25 to 35 minutes, until firm in center. Turn onto a wire rack to cool.

2. Make praline as for Figs with Praline (see page 87); crush with a rolling pin. To make filling, put apricots and soaking liquid in a saucepan, bring to a boil, cover and cook 15 minutes. Drain, chop and cool. Whip cream until thick; set two-thirds aside. Fold apricots and 2 tablespoons praline into remaining cream.

3. Split cake in half horizontally and sandwich together with the apricot and praline cream. Spread a thin layer of cream over side of cake and coat with praline. Cover top with a thin layer of cream.

Put remaining cream in a pastry bag fitted with a large fluted tip and pipe lines at 1/2-inch intervals on cake. Spoon remaining praline in between. Decorate with candied apricot slices.

Makes 8 servings.

Greek Walnut Cake

1/2 cup butter or margarine, softened
1/2 cup light brown sugar
2 eggs
1-1/2 cups self-rising flour, sifted
1-1/3 cups walnut pieces, ground
2/3 cup plain yogurt
SYRUP:
3/4 cup sugar
1/2 cup water
1 teaspoon ground cinnamon
COFFEE CREAM:
2/3 cup whipping cream
2 tablespoons Kahlua or Tia Maria liqueur
TO DECORATE:
2 tablespoons chopped walnuts

1. Preheat oven to 350F (175C). Grease a deep 8-inch-round cake pan.

In a medium-size bowl, cream butter or margarine and brown sugar together until light and fluffy. Beat in eggs one at a time, adding a tablespoon of flour with each one. Mix remaining flour and ground walnuts together and fold into the mixture alternately with the yogurt.

2. Turn cake mixture into prepared pan and bake 45 to 50 minutes, until the center springs back when pressed. Prick the surface all over with a skewer.

3. To make syrup, in a saucepan, heat sugar, 1/2 cup water and cinnamon until sugar has dissolved, then boil 2 minutes. Gradually pour syrup over the warm cake. Cool in pan.

To make coffee cream, whip cream and liqueur together until it holds its shape.

Serve the cake in wedges, topped with the cream and sprinkled with chopped walnuts.

Makes 10 servings.

Glacé Fruit Cake

1/2 cup plus 2 tablespoons butter or margarine, softened
1 cup light brown sugar
3 eggs
1-3/4 cups whole-wheat flour
1 teaspoon each mixed spice and ground cinnamon
1-1/2 cups raisins
1 cup golden raisins
2/3 cup glacé cherries, halved
2 tablespoons sherry
TO FINISH:
3 ounces pecans
2 ounces each glacé cherries and pineapple pieces,
halved
1 (1-inch) piece of angelica, cut into strips
2 tablespoons apricot jam
2 teaspoons lemon juice

1. Grease a deep 8-inch round cake pan and line bottom and side with a triple layer of greased waxed paper. Preheat oven to 325F (165C).

2. In a bowl, cream butter or margarine and sugar together until light and fluffy. Beat in eggs one at a time, adding a tablespoon of flour with each of the last 2 eggs. Add remaining flour with spices and fold into the mixture with the raisins, glacé cherries and sherry.

3. Turn mixture into prepared pan and decorate with nuts, glacé fruits and angelica. Bake 1 hour; reduce temperature to 300F (150C) and bake about 1-1/2 hours, until a skewer inserted into the center of the cake comes out clean. Turn onto a wire rack to cool.

Heat jam and lemon juice together in a small saucepan over low heat until jam has melted; sieve, reheat and brush over glacé fruit.

Makes 8 servings.

Portuguese Almond Cake

6 tablespoons butter, softened
1/2 cup sugar
2 eggs
2 tablespoons ground almonds
1 cup self-rising flour, sifted
2 tablespoons milk
Few drops almond extract
TOPPING:
6 tablespoons butter
1/2 cup light brown sugar
3 tablespoons milk
3/4 cup slivered almonds, toasted

1. Preheat oven to 350F (175C). Grease and flour an 8-1/2-inch fluted flan pan.

In a medium-size bowl, cream butter and sugar together until light and fluffy. Beat in eggs, one at a time, adding ground almonds with second egg. Carefully fold in flour with a metal spoon; when almost incorporated, fold in milk and almond extract. Turn mixture into the prepared flan pan and smooth the surface. Bake 25 to 30 minutes, until firm in the center. Leave in the pan.

2. To make topping, put butter, brown sugar and milk in a small saucepan and heat gently until sugar has dissolved. Bring to a boil and cook 8 minutes, stirring occasionally, until a little of the mixture forms a soft ball when dropped into cold water. Stir in slivered almonds.

3. Pour almond topping over warm cake, spreading to the edge. Cool in the pan, then remove and cut into slices, using a serrated knife.

Makes 8 servings.

Walnut & Red Currant Roll

3 eggs
1/2 cup sugar
1/2 cup all-purpose flour, sifted
2/3 cup walnut pieces, ground
1 tablespoon hot water
Powdered sugar
FILLING:
3/4 cup whipping cream
1 tablespoon framboise liqueur or kirsch
3 ounces red currants
3 ounces raspberries
1 tablespoon powdered sugar

1. Preheat oven to 400F (205C). Grease and line a 12" x 8" jellyroll pan.

Whisk eggs and sugar together, using an electric mixer, until very thick and creamy. Carefully fold in flour and walnuts, adding water when almost incorporated. Turn mixture into prepared pan and bake 8 to 10 minutes, until cake springs back when lightly pressed in the center.

2. Put a sheet of waxed paper on a work surface and sprinkle liberally with powdered sugar. Turn cake out onto the paper; remove paper. Trim off crisp edges of cake, then roll up with the paper inside the cake. Put on a wire rack, with end underneath, and cool.

To make filling, whip cream with liqueur. Set aside 4 stems of red currants. Strip remaining red currants from stalks and add to cream with raspberries and powdered sugar.

3. Unroll cake and spread cream mixture over, then roll up again with end underneath; place on a serving dish. Decorate with reserved red currants to serve.

Makes 8 servings.

Almond & Chocolate Cake

4 ounces semisweet chocolate, in pieces
2 tablespoons water
1/2 cup butter, softened
3/4 cup light brown sugar
4 eggs, separated
1-1/4 cups ground almonds
1/2 cup all-purpose flour, sifted
TOPPING:
2 tablespoons milk
1 tablespoon vegetable oil
6 ounces semisweet chocolate, in pieces

1. Preheat oven to 325F (165C). Grease and line an 8-inch-round cake pan.

Put chocolate and 2 tablespoons water in a saucepan and heat very gently until melted. In a bowl, cream butter and sugar together until light and fluffy. Beat in egg yolks. Mix in warm, melted chocolate, then stir in ground almonds and flour.

2. Whisk egg whites until fairly stiff; fold 2 tablespoons into chocolate mixture to lighten, then carefully fold in remainder. Turn mixture into prepared pan and bake 60 to 65 minutes, until a skewer inserted into the center of the cake comes out clean. Turn onto a wire rack to cool.

3. To make topping, in a small saucepan combine milk, oil and 5 ounces of the chocolate and stir over low heat until melted; stir until smooth. Pour over cake, spread evenly over top and side and leave until set.

Melt remaining chocolate in a small bowl over a saucepan of warm water; put into a paper pastry bag. Using a sharp knife, mark the cake into 8 portions. Snip off the end of the pastry bag and drizzle a zigzag design over each section.

Makes 8 servings.

Pear & Chocolate Cake

4 ounces dried pears
6 ounces graham crackers
6 ounces semisweet chocolate, in pieces
1 cup chopped hazelnuts, toasted
2 tablespoons brandy
TOPPING:
1/4 cup whipping cream
1 ounce semisweet chocolate, melted

1. Grease and line an 8-inch-round cake pan. Put pears in a bowl and cover with boiling water. Soak 1 hour, then drain thoroughly and chop, reserving 1 tablespoon liquid. Put graham crackers in a plastic bag and crush with a rolling pin.
2. Put the chocolate and reserved liquid in a saucepan and heat gently until melted. Add chopped pears to saucepan with hazelnuts, crumbs and the brandy. Stir well to mix thorough-ly, then turn into prepared pan, smoothing top with a palette knife.
3. Refrigerate until set. Turn out onto a serving plate and remove paper. Whip cream and spread even-ly over top of cake to edge. Put melted chocolate in a paper pastry bag, snip off end with scissors, and drizzle lines of chocolate all over the cream.

Makes 6 to 8 servings.

Pignola

RICH PASTRY:
1 cup all-purpose flour
1/4 cup butter
1/4 cup sugar
2 egg yolks
FILLING:
1/2 cup butter, softened
1/2 cup sugar
3 eggs
1/4 cup all-purpose flour, sifted
1-1/4 cups ground almonds
Few drops of almond extract
3/4 cup pine nuts
2 tablespoons honey, warmed

1. To make pastry, sift flour onto a marble slab or cool work surface. Make a well in the center and put butter, sugar and egg yolks into well. Using fingertips of one hand, work these ingredients together, then draw in flour. Knead lightly until smooth, then cover and refrigerate 1 hour.

On a lightly floured surface, roll out pastry very thinly and use to line a 9-1/2-inch fluted flan ring. Prick pastry bottom and refrigerate 20 minutes. Preheat oven to 375F (190C).

2. To make filling, cream butter and sugar together in a bowl until light and fluffy. Beat in eggs one at a time, adding flour with second egg, ground almonds and almond extract with third egg.

3. Turn into pastry shell, smooth surface and sprinkle pine nuts over the top. Put on a baking sheet so that heat transfers more quickly to bottom of flan and cooks the pastry. Bake 30 minutes, until golden. Brush with honey and return to oven 5 minutes. Transfer to a wire rack to cool.

Makes 8 servings.

Hazelnut Ganache

6 tablespoons butter or margarine, softened
1/3 cup light brown sugar
1/2 cup all-purpose flour, sifted
2/3 cup hazelnuts, ground and toasted
GANACHE CREAM:
5 ounces semisweet chocolate, in small pieces
2 tablespoons butter
1/2 cup whipping cream
1 tablespoon brandy
TOPPING:
2 ounces semisweet chocolate
2/3 cup whipping cream
Powdered sugar to sprinkle

1. Preheat oven to 325F (165C). Grease a shallow 8-inch fluted flan pan.

In a bowl, cream butter and sugar together until light and fluffy; stir in flour and hazelnuts and mix to a firm dough, using your hand. On a floured surface, knead lightly until smooth, then roll out into a 7-inch round and press into bottom of prepared pan. Bake 35 to 40 minutes; cool in the pan.

2. To make ganache cream, put chocolate, butter and cream in a small saucepan and heat gently until melted; stir in brandy. Spread over hazelnut crust, smoothing the top with a spatula. Refrigerate until set and firm.

3. To make chocolate scrolls, melt chocolate and pour onto a marble slab or cold surface; spread evenly with a spatula. When it begins to set, push a long, sharp thin-bladed knife across chocolate at a slight angle. Use a slight sawing action to obtain long, thin scrolls.

Remove cake from flan pan and put onto a serving plate. Whip cream and spread over the top to come neatly to the edge. Arrange scrolls on top and sprinkle with powdered sugar to serve.

Makes 8 servings.

Fig & Pear Strudel

4 ounces dried figs
4 ounces dried pears
1 tablespoon sugar
2 teaspoons ground cinnamon
1/2 teaspoon ground cloves
3 sheets filo pastry
2 tablespoons butter, melted
1/2 cup chopped almonds
Powdered sugar, to sprinkle

1. Preheat oven to 375F (190C). Grease a baking sheet.

Put figs and pears in a bowl, cover with boiling water and soak 3 hours; drain thoroughly. Remove stems from figs, then chop fruit coarsely and return to bowl. Mix sugar and spices together and stir into fruit.

2. Lay a sheet of filo pastry on a work surface and brush with butter. Lay a second sheet on top, brush with butter; top with remaining sheet and brush with butter. Spread fruit filling down one long side of pastry; sprinkle with three-quarters of the almonds and roll up like a jellyroll. Cut in half.

3. Put on prepared baking sheet, brush with butter and sprinkle with remaining almonds. Bake 25 to 30 minutes, until golden-brown. Sprinkle with powdered sugar and cut into slices.

Serve warm or cold, with whipped cream if desired.

Makes 8 servings.

Hazelnut Boats

RICH PASTRY:
1 cup all-purpose flour
1/4 cup butter
1/4 cup sugar
2 egg yolks
FILLING:
1/3 cup light brown sugar
2 tablespoons honey
1/4 cup butter
1 tablespoon water
1-1/4 cups hazelnuts, toasted

1. To make pastry, sift flour onto a marble slab or cool work surface. Make a well in the center and put butter, sugar and egg yolks into well. Using fingertips of one hand, work these ingredients together, then draw in flour. Knead lightly until smooth, then refrigerate 1 hour.

On a lightly floured surface, roll out pastry thinly and use to line 12 (3-inch) barquette (boat-shaped) molds. Prick bottoms and refrigerate 15 minutes. Preheat oven to 375F (190C). Press a square of foil into each mold and bake "blind" 8 to 10 min-utes, until golden. Remove foil and cool.

2. To make filling, in a heavy-bottom pan, heat sugar, honey, butter and 1 tablespoon cold water over low heat until dissolved; boil 5 to 7 minutes, until a little dropped into cold water forms a soft ball. Stir hazelnuts into syrup.

3. Spoon filling into pastry cases before it begins to set. Cool, then remove from molds.

Makes 12 servings.

Hazelnut & Chocolate Cookies

1/2 cup butter, softened
1/4 cup sugar
1-1/4 cups all-purpose flour, sifted
2/3 cup hazelnuts, ground and toasted
3 tablespoons chocolate and hazelnut spread
2 ounces semisweet chocolate, melted

1. Preheat oven to 350F (175C). In a medium-size bowl, cream butter and sugar together until light and fluffy. Add flour and hazelnuts and work together with your hand to form a smooth dough. On a lightly floured surface, roll out thinly and cut into rounds, using a 2-inch plain cutter. Place on a baking sheet and bake 15 minutes, until golden-brown. Transfer to a wire rack to cool.
2. Sandwich cookies together in pairs with chocolate and hazelnut spread; place on a wire rack. Coat cookie tops with half the melted chocolate, spreading evenly with a spatula. Leave to set.
3. Place remaining chocolate in a paper pastry bag, snip off the end and drizzle chocolate over cookies to decorate.

Makes 20 servings.

Fig & Banana Slices

6 ounces dried figs, chopped
4 ounces dried bananas, chopped
2 tablespoons brandy
6 tablespoons butter or margarine, softened
1/2 cup light brown sugar
2 eggs
1 cup whole-wheat flour
1 teaspoon baking powder
1/4 teaspoon salt
1 cup chopped Brazil nuts

1. Preheat oven to 350F (175C). Grease and line an 11" x 7" baking pan.

Put figs and bananas in a medium-size bowl, sprinkle with brandy and soak 1 hour.

In another bowl, cream butter and sugar together until pale and fluffy. Beat in eggs, one at a time, adding a little flour with the second egg. Add remaining flour, baking powder, salt, figs, bananas and all but 2 table-spoons of the nuts and mix thoroughly to a soft consistency.

2. Turn mixture into prepared pan and sprinkle remaining nuts over the top. Bake 30 to 35 minutes, until firm in the center.

3. Remove from pan carefully and place on a wire rack. When cold, cut into slices with a sharp knife.

Makes 18 to 20 servings.

Pickled Prunes

2-1/2 cups pitted prunes
5 cups tea
3 slices fresh gingerroot
Pared peel of 1 lemon
4 cloves
8 black peppercorns
1 dried chile
1/3 cup light brown sugar
2/3 cup red wine vinegar

1. Put prunes in a large bowl, pour tea over them and stir. Leave to soak overnight.

Put prunes and soaking liquid in a saucepan. Tie gingerroot, lemon peel, cloves, peppercorns and chile together in cheesecloth. Add to prunes with sugar and vinegar.

2. Heat gently until the sugar has dissolved, bring to a boil, then cover and simmer gently 10 to 15 minutes, until the prunes are tender. Remove cheesecloth bag.

3. Spoon prunes into sterilized jars and pour over syrup. Seal with a lid, cool and refrigerate until used.

Makes 2 (1-lb.) jars.

Note: The prunes can be used after 24 hours, but will keep for up to 8 weeks stored in the refrigerator. They are delicious served with cold pork or other cold meats, and are particularly useful at Christmas.

Spiced Apricots

1-3/4 cups dried apricots
2 tablespoons white wine vinegar
1/2 cup white wine
1 (2-inch) piece cinnamon stick
8 black peppercorns
4 cloves
1/4 cup sugar

1. Put apricots in a medium-size bowl, cover with water and soak overnight.

Drain apricots, reserving liquid in a measure; make up to 1-1/4 cups with water. Put measured liquid in a saucepan with the vinegar, wine, spices and sugar; cook over low heat until the sugar has dissolved. Bring to a boil, then reduce heat and simmer 5 minutes. Add apricots, cover and simmer 20 minutes.

2. Remove apricots with a slotted spoon and put in a sterilized jar.

3. Boil the syrup rapidly to reduce to approximately 2/3 cup. Strain, then pour over fruit and seal with a lid. Cover and refrigerate up to 8 weeks until used.

Makes 1 pound.

Note: This tasty preserve goes well with cold meats, particularly ham, pork and chicken.

Stuffed Dates

1 pound dates
ALMOND PASTE:
1/3 cup ground almonds
1-1/2 tablespoons powdered sugar, sifted
2 tablespoons plus 2 teaspoons granulated sugar
1 large egg yolk
1 teaspoon lemon juice
Few drops almond extract
APRICOT & PISTACHIO FILLING:
2/3 cup apricots, soaked overnight and drained
1/4 cup pistachios, finely chopped
1 teaspoon honey
3 to 4 cardamom pods, shelled and chopped

1. Cut along the length of each date and remove the pit.

2. To make almond paste, mix ground almonds, powdered sugar and half the granulated sugar in a bowl. Make a well in the center, add egg yolk, lemon juice and almond extract; mix to a smooth firm paste.

Divide almond paste into 30 pieces and shape into ovals. Use to stuff half the dates, reshaping them to show the almond paste. Put remaining granulated sugar in a small plastic bag and shake dates, two at a time, in the sugar until completely coated.

3. To make apricot and pistachio filling, cook apricots in simmering water 15 minutes; drain, and chop finely. Put in a bowl with pistachios, honey and chopped cardamom seeds. Mix to a paste then, using dampened hands, form into ovals. Use to stuff the remaining dates.

Makes 60.

Hazelnut Dates: Use finely ground hazelnuts instead of almonds.

Apricot Drops: Shape the apricot and pistachio mixture into small balls, the size of a marble, and shake in 3 tablespoons ground almonds or chopped pistachios.

Apricot & Pistachio Rolls

1 cup dried apricots
2 teaspoons grated orange peel
1/2 teaspoon grated nutmeg
1 tablespoon brandy
1 teaspoon honey
4 sheets filo pastry
2 tablespoons butter, melted
2 tablespoons chopped pistachios
Powdered sugar to sprinkle

  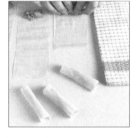

1. Put apricots in a small bowl, cover with water and soak overnight. Put apricots in a saucepan with 2/3 cup of the soaking liquid. Simmer gently 15 minutes, then drain thoroughly and chop finely. Stir in orange peel, nutmeg, brandy and honey; cool.

2. Cut filo pastry into 3-inch widths across the length of the sheet and pile on top of each other. Cover with a clean towel to prevent pastry from drying out.

3. Preheat oven to 375F (190C). Take 3 strips of pastry and brush the top two-thirds of each with butter. Put a spoonful of the apricot mixture on unbuttered third of each pastry strip. Roll up like a jellyroll, leaving the ends open; put onto a baking sheet. Repeat with remaining pastry and filling.

Brush rolls with butter, sprinkle with pistachios and bake 12 to 15 minutes, until golden-brown. Cool, then sprinkle with powdered sugar.

Makes 24.

Chocolate Clusters & Orangettes

CHOCOLATE CLUSTERS:
6 ounces semisweet chocolate, in pieces
1 tablespoon butter
3/4 cup hazelnuts, toasted
3/4 cup raisins
ORANGETTES:
6 ounces semisweet chocolate
1 tablespoon butter
4 ounces large orange peel strips

1. To make chocolate clusters, put chocolate and butter in a heatproof bowl over a saucepan of hot water and heat gently until melted, being careful not to allow any water into the chocolate.

2. Stir hazelnuts and raisins into melted chocolate. Put teaspoonfuls of the mixture into small paper cases. Leave to set.

3. To make orangettes, melt chocolate and butter as above. Using a skewer, dip each piece of peel into melted chocolate; allow excess chocolate to drip into a bowl. Place on a baking sheet lined with waxed paper and leave until set. Peel off carefully and serve piled on a glass dish.

Makes 24 clusters and 50 orangettes.

Papaya & Pistachio Clusters: Use milk chocolate instead of semisweet chocolate and substitute dried papaya and roasted shelled pistachios for raisins and hazelnuts.

Pistachio Florentines

6 tablespoons butter
1/4 cup dark corn syrup
1/4 cup all-purpose flour
1/2 cup pistachios, coarsely chopped
1/2 cup slivered almonds, coarsely chopped
1/3 cup glacé cherries, coarsely chopped
1 teaspoon lemon juice
4 ounces semisweet chocolate, melted

1. Preheat oven to 350F (175C). Line 2 baking sheets with parchment paper.

In a pan, heat butter and syrup gently until melted. Stir in flour, nuts, cherries and lemon juice.

2. Put small mounds of the mixture, the size of a cherry, well apart on prepared baking sheets and flatten with a fork. Bake 6 to 8 minutes. Leave on the baking sheets 1 minute, then transfer to a wire rack to cool.

3. Spread chocolate over flat underside of each florentine. Put cookies, chocolate side up, on a wire rack and mark the chocolate into wavy lines with a fork. Leave until set.

Makes about 50.

Variation: Replace glacé cherries with 2 tablespoons chopped dates and 1 ounce chopped dried apricots.